Diesel Days

Devon and Cornwall

Diesel Days

Devon and Cornwall

John Vaughan

Ian Allan
PUBLISHING

Front cover: Disturbing the still early-morning air on a cold winter's day Class 37 No 37 247 climbs slowly into Liskeard station with a long rake of empty china-clay wagons destined for the English China Clay works at Moorswater. *Author*

Back cover (upper): This excellent example of a GWR/WR signal gantry, with a fine array of lower-quadrant semaphores, was located at the up end of Newton Abbot station. Framed by the gantry is a Paddington–Penzance train headed by a Class 47/4 in Rail blue. *Author*

Back cover (lower): With a stormy sky as a backdrop, one of the handsome but in this view tired-looking Class 52 'Western' diesel-hydraulics pauses at Liskeard station in 1974 with a train bound for the Eastern Region. The signalbox survives today, but locomotive, Mk 1 coaches, down siding and down station building have all disappeared from the scene. *Author*

First published 2005
ISBN 0 7110 3040 5

© John Vaughan 2005

Published by Ian Allan Publishing

an imprint of Ian Allan Publishing Ltd, Hersham, Surrey KT12 4RG.

Printed in England by Ian Allan Printing Ltd, Hersham, Surrey KT12 4RG.

Code: 0506/B

Above: The remarkable main-line rail link between Devon and Cornwall is Brunel's impressive Royal Albert Bridge of 1859 vintage. For nearly 150 years the single track across the structure has linked the two counties. The only other surviving railway connection between Devon and Cornwall is the viaduct across the River Tamar at Calstock, on the Gunnislake branch. Easing the four-coach 14.30 Plymouth–Par local across the bridge on 21 November 1983 is No 50 005 *Collingwood,* seen through a 200mm Nikkor telephoto lens. *Author*

Half-title: A delightful backwater in the county of Cornwall that still has rail traffic to photograph is Coombe Junction, near Liskeard. Seen from the platform of the small halt, Class 37 No 37 299 emerges from the narrow bridge over the line to Moorswater to collect more china-clay wagons from Liskeard station on 16 April 1981. In the background is the 150ft-high Moorswater Viaduct, which carries the main line from Plymouth to Penzance. The freight line is now heavily overgrown and used only by cement traffic. *Author*

Title page: An all-time classic trackside structure in Cornwall, and one that encapsulates Cornwall's industrial past, is the abandoned engine house at Hallenbeagle mine, near Scorrier. In a scene that can never be recaptured with a camera, Class 50 No 50 009 *Conqueror* heads westward with Mk 1 stock constituting a Brighton–Penzance working on the afternoon of 13 August 1983. Although the mine closed a century ago a siding and signalbox were located here until 1964. *Author*

Contents

Arguably the most scenic and certainly the best-known stretch of railway line
in the county of Devon (if not the UK) is the famous 'sea wall' section between
Starcross and Teignmouth. Countless thousands of photographs have been taken
in the area since the beginning of photography and the days of the broad gauge.
Leaving Teignmouth on 23 May 1981 with a long (13-coach) up buffet-car express
is Class 47 No 47 484, fittingly named *Isambard Kingdom Brunel*. *Author*

Introduction

In 1955 the British Transport Commission published its Modernisation Plan. Except for older documentation relating to the 1948 Nationalisation of Britain's railways this was the first major, post-World War 2, forward-looking policy document setting out the future direction for the nation's railways. As mentioned in more detail in the following 'Background' text, in addition to addressing infrastructure generally, ranging from freight wagons and signalling to track improvement and electrification proposals, the BTC initially allocated a total of £150 million for the procurement of diesel power. In values that are now 50 years old this was a considerable amount of money.

The BTC made an announcement within the Plan that was to have a very considerable impact on the Western Region of British Railways, particularly the counties of Devon and Cornwall (and, incidentally, the Western Section of the Southern Region, including main lines to Weymouth and Exeter), in that the *total* dieselisation of all lines west of Newton Abbot was proposed. Prior to 1955 there had been occasional special train incursions into Devon and Cornwall by GWR diesel railcars in the 1930s, a few shunting locomotives for engineers' and industrial use and in the early 1950s the five original main-line diesel locomotives from the English Electric stable, working between Waterloo and Exeter Central. Under the new proposals it was envisaged that a total of 130 diesel locomotives would be required to work all trains throughout Devon and Cornwall.

As explained in the 'Background' section the design, ordering and building of the various types of diesel locomotives was heavily influenced by the 1955 Diesel Pilot Scheme, which was linked to the Modernisation Plan. Political pressures influenced the ordering of a number of Pilot Scheme diesel locomotives from a variety of British manufacturers that were in need of new sources of revenue. The direct importation of tried and tested designs from (particularly) the USA and Germany was largely ignored. The only exceptions to this policy were diesel engines and transmissions (particularly from Switzerland and Germany) that were manufactured in the UK under licence, with the relevant foreign companies working in conjunction with British firms. Although interesting from the railway-enthusiast perspective, BR's objective of 'gaining experience of diesel operation in British conditions before standardising types for mass production' was, in the eyes of many, a costly and unnecessary process. Part of this ill-fated procurement policy was the excessive focus on low-powered machinery in the sub-1,600hp category.

In 1958 the first of the original five 2,000hp A1A-A1A 'Warship' locomotives (later known as Class 41), No D600, arrived in the West, and this was followed by sister locomotives D601-4. Examples of the lighter 2,000hp B-B 'Warships' (Classes 42 and 43) and also the 1,000/1,100hp 'D63xx' B-Bs (Class 22) gradually arrived in Devon and Cornwall between 1958 and 1962. It was significant that all these locomotives were diesel-hydraulics, as distinct from the diesel-electric types that were then being tested on other regions, as potentially viable alternatives. The policy issues behind the adoption by the Western Region of a diesel-hydraulic policy are detailed in the 'Background' section. The diesel-hydraulic theme was continued by the introduction in 1962/3 of the more powerful 2,700hp C-C 'Westerns' (Class 52). In the meantime, at the start of the 1960s diesel multiple-units arrived in the West to take over many (but not all) local and branch-line services. Although the majority of the 1,700hp 'Hymek' B-B (Class 35) diesel-hydraulic locomotives were allocated elsewhere on the Western Region, they too filtered down to Devon and Cornwall from 1963, and some were later allocated to Newton Abbot and Plymouth Laira.

Although Newton Abbot and Laira motive-power depots were eventually modernised and substantially rebuilt to accommodate the new generation of diesel locomotives, initially the diesel-hydraulics had to share steam-age accommodation with traditional GWR/WR motive power, as locomotive delivery was outpacing the construction of maintenance facilities. In the early days a couple of roads in the steam sheds were dedicated to diesel traction, but the relatively dirty environment was not conducive to the maintenance of sophisticated machinery, and new structures offering more clinical surroundings were established by the early 1960s. Far fewer depots were required in the diesel era, and, although depots such as St Blazey survived, those at Penzance, Truro and Exmouth Junction were either closed or reduced in status, while eventually even Exeter Riverside became little more than a stabling point. Most sub-sheds and small depots on branch lines closed completely.

At this juncture it is important to point out that while the Western Region was conducting all of this diesel-procurement activity some of the railway lines in Devon and Cornwall were in the hands of the Southern Region, which had its own diesel-traction policy. After many boundary changes the Western Region eventually assumed 'ownership' of all lines west of Wilton Junction, near Salisbury, but in the early days of dieselisation, until 1964/5, Southern Region steam locomotives still worked the majority of Waterloo–Salisbury–Exeter services. The Southern Region's BRCW Bo-Bos (Class 33) also worked regularly into Devon, especially from 1971, when they replaced 'Warships' on the Waterloo–Exeter route.

The BTC's objective of ending steam haulage was quickly achieved, and by 1964 steam had been banished from the two primary 'West Country' counties. By this time also a number of decisions had been made regarding a BR standard diesel locomotive, and although the Western Region had nailed its colours to the diesel-hydraulic mast the British Railways Board's motive-power chiefs had decided that diesel-electric locomotives represented the way forward. As a consequence Class 47s, Class 45s/46s and Class 25s gradually found themselves either allocated to West Country depots or working through trains into Devon and Cornwall.

It is amazing now to realise that the selection of the diesel-electrics as standard had such an immediate and profound impact on the ranks of the diesel-hydraulics. As early as 1967 the original 'Warships' had all been withdrawn, by 1971 the small Class 22s were extinct, and (almost unbelievably) by the end of 1972 the last of the 71 B-B 'Warships' of Classes 42 and 43 was only days away from the scrap line. The Class 35 'Hymeks' soldiered on until 1975, and the last of the magnificent Class 52 'Westerns' survived until February 1977. In total some 309 main-line diesel-hydraulic locomotives were in operation on the Western Region for a maximum period of 19 years, some having a lifespan of as little as six years. It was a unique and wonderful era, and happily over a dozen examples have been preserved, albeit without examples of Classes 22, 41 and 43.

In November 1973 an English Electric Class 50 arrived at Plymouth's Laira depot for crew training, and in the subsequent years and until the very beginning of the 1990s most of the class were regular performers in Devon and Cornwall. The Class 50s replaced the last of the diesel-hydraulics before being ousted, albeit over a period of many years, by the increasing number of Inter-City 125 Class 253 High Speed Train units. IC125 units arrived in the Duchy of Cornwall for crew training in 1979, and they were soon put to work on the prestigious 'Golden Hind' and 'Cornish Riviera' expresses. Also in 1979 the ubiquitous but reliable Class 37s arrived and replaced the diesel-electric Class 25s, and from 1985 — about the time the last of the Class 46s was being withdrawn — Class 45 'Peaks' were effectively banned west of Bristol, bringing to an end sightings of these 136-ton, 2,500hp 1Co-Co1 monsters. Classes 31 and 33 were regular visitors to Devon and occasionally Cornwall, but other classes appeared only on special trains or as 'one-off' workings. By the mid-1980s the railways were changing, with new-generation diesel multiple-units appearing in increasing numbers and the prospect of sectorisation and privatisation looming.

This volume covers a period of well over 30 years, from October 1951 until the end of 1985 — a time when good old British Railways operated the national railway system, albeit with the aid of significant government subsidy. By and large the nationalised organisation delivered the goods, even though the network had been savaged in the 1960s and freight traffic had been in terminal decline for years! For the diesel-hydraulic fans the heyday of 'Diesel Days' would have been *circa* 1966, after the end of steam but before large-scale incursions of diesel-electric types, while for the general diesel-locomotive enthusiast the optimum would perhaps have been 1975/6, when no fewer than five Type 4 classes were working the main lines and some diesel-hydraulics were still extant.

What has been so striking in compiling this volume has been not only the significant motive-power changes that have taken place since the mid-1980s but also the rationalisation of the entire railway infrastructure. Many lines and stations have closed, some traffic flows have ceased altogether, rolling stock has seen radical changes and signalling and station buildings have been systematically modernised. It is hard to believe that perishables, parcels, post, cement, coal, fertiliser and wagonload freight traffic of every description, ranging from beer and fish to calcified seaweed and gunpowder, have gone forever. Even the range of china-clay traffic has diminished as worldwide demand and corporate upheavals take their toll. As a result of all these changes today's railway photographer, standing on an overbridge in either Devon or Cornwall, waiting for a locomotive-hauled train, has much leaner 'pickings' than had the photographer of yesteryear. Even when a locomotive appears, a freight train is likely to be hauled by either a Class 66 or a Class 60, and a passenger working by one of the few remaining Class 47s, with the occasional Class 67 thrown in. There is always room for surprises, such as recalled Class 37s being rostered for some St Blazey–Meldon Quarry ballast workings in 2003/4, but otherwise locomotive variety is now limited.

The early days of the diesel-hydraulics aside, the current photographer undoubtedly scores when it comes to train liveries. From 1966 BR's diesel-locomotive fleet, with a handful of exceptions, was painted in a rather drab all-blue livery with all-yellow cab ends, which although acceptable in ex-works condition became rather a depressing colour when either dirty or weathered. Fortunately many of the locomotives featured herein were painted in green, maroon or even desert-sand liveries, with no yellow warning panel at all or only a small warning panel. Passenger coaches could be maroon, 'blood and custard', chocolate and cream, blue and grey or just plain blue. However, towards the end of the period covered by this book only the last two of these alternatives were commonplace, only special or Royal trains escaping the standard BR livery!

Rather than sticking rigidly to a collection of photographs in strict chronological order, or dividing Devon and Cornwall into a large number of arbitrary geographical areas, I have presented the photographs on a thematic basis, whether it be class of locomotive, type of train, location, livery, weather, railway structure or other common identifier. I hope that this form of presentation helps to maintain interest and gives a varied and balanced view of the immense variety of the complete railway scene in Devon and Cornwall and the significant changes that took place during the 1951-85 period.

Although I did not commence my extensive and frequent travels to Devon and particularly Cornwall until 1969, the railways of the far South West were almost to become an obsession in subsequent years, many thousands of frames being exposed in capturing this period of railway history on film. I am privileged in having been afforded the opportunity on many occasions to record the passing railway scene in the South West in books and magazines, but this title is different in that it exclusively covers a period of great changes in modern traction, and thus nostalgia abounds. Having witnessed the passing of steam on the Western Region (the first to eliminate steam completely) in 1965, I now find it strange to be recalling the passing of many classes of diesel locomotive that shared the Western rails with their coal-burning ancestors in the dying years of steam.

The early days in particular could not have been so well illustrated without the assistance of many photographer colleagues and friends, and I thank each of them (in the 'Acknowledge-ments' section on the last page) for their kind co-operation. Wherever possible I have tried to use previously unpublished photographs, although a handful of unique or historic shots and a couple of outstanding prints published long ago may have crept in. It is the overall result that counts, and I hope that this volume provides the reader with many happy hours of wallowing in the pleasant nostalgia provided by an era that is now modern but ancient!

The book is dedicated to my old friend John Hicks, as an expression of gratitude for his company on so many visits to the West Country.

John A. M. Vaughan
Goring-by-Sea, West Sussex
January 2005

Background

Prior to the 1950s steam traction had reigned supreme in Devon and Cornwall for well over 100 years. For the majority of that time rail services had been in the hands of either the Great Western Railway/BR Western Region or the London & South Western Railway/Southern Railway/BR Southern Region (or their respective constituent companies). The GWR and the LSWR/SR were largely independent of each other, although there were a few stretches of track where the two shared running rights. From the 1950s to the 1970s there were many changes of boundary, but by the end of the 1960s all lines in Devon and Cornwall were in the hands of the Western Region,

and the only significant anachronism from an otherwise all-Western Region show was the former LSWR/SR main line from Waterloo to Exeter. Even that was later to become part of the Western Region, at least from Wilton Junction (near Salisbury) westward. Following the Beeching era major chunks of the former LSWR/SR network in Cornwall and Devon, including lines to Wadebridge, Padstow, Bodmin North, Bude, Oke-hampton, Ilfracombe, Torrington, Budleigh Salterton, Sidmouth, Seaton and Lyme Regis, were all closed under the auspices of the former rival company, this network becoming known as the 'Withered Arm'. In addition the former LSWR main line between Exeter and Plymouth was closed completely from Meldon Junction (near Okehampton) to Bere Alston in May 1968.

The former GWR lines were not immune from closure, and during the period covered by this book (from *c*1951 to 1985) dozens of branches and secondary lines closed, in both South Devon and Cornwall. Some closed in the pre-diesel era, but, reflecting the national picture, most had their services withdrawn during the 1960s. Some of the freight-only lines were not abandoned until the 1970s and 1980s, when they succumbed as a result of the downturn in the railway freight business. China-clay lines in Cornwall proved to be particularly vulnerable, especially those serving older installations. Some of the so-called 'holiday lines' including those serving Exmouth, Barnstaple, Looe, Newquay and St Ives, survived against the odds, but others,

Excepting a handful of internal-combustion-engined industrial shunters and pre-World War 2 GWR railcar movements, diesel days in Devon and Cornwall commenced in October 1951, when the second of two SR English Electric main-line locomotives headed the 1pm Waterloo–Exeter/Ilfracombe/Plymouth express. The origins of the 1,750hp 1Co-Co1 locomotives dated back to the days of the Southern Railway, but it took many years to develop original ideas into actual locomotives. The interesting looks and the mechanical components of No 10202, seen here leaving Woking, can be attributed to O. V. S. Bulleid, whereas electrical components owed more to C. M. Cook, the SR's Chief Electrical Engineer. A third, more powerful locomotive of the type was built later. *Author's collection*

particularly those to Kingswear, Brixham, Kingsbridge, Perranporth, Bodmin General and Helston, failed to beat the system. Several of these closed lines are illustrated within these pages.

The history of diesel traction in Devon and Cornwall in terms of the main railway system (as distinct from industrial use) goes back to the 1930s, when, on a number of occasions, the GWR's streamlined railcars worked through Devon and into the Royal Duchy. For example, No 10 worked to Newquay on a parcels-exhibition special in the late 1930s, another railcar worked to both Looe and Kingswear before World War 2, and in 1938 one of the streamliners was seen at St Budeaux. In another instance a GWR railcar worked to Newquay with a bell-ringer's special. (I wonder what the signalman's bell code was for that working!)

The first appearances of main-line diesel locomotives in the West had nothing whatsoever to do with the GWR/WR but arose from postwar development plans prepared by the Southern Railway. When World War 2 ended in 1945 the 'big four' railway companies were giving consideration to alternative forms of motive power. It was the SR that took the lead, and in 1946 a party of senior officials visited the USA, the undisputed world leader in the production and operation of diesel-electric traction. The findings from their visit obviously made a deep and favourable impression, because in the latter part of 1946 the SR announced its intention to build three 1,600hp diesel locomotives for service between Waterloo and Exeter. However, progress over the following years was slow, and in the meantime, in 1948, the railways were nationalised. While there was to be some regional discretion, the entire system came under the control of the central British Railways Board/British Transport Commission. In the meantime, in 1947, the London, Midland & Scottish Railway had also shown interest in diesel traction, collaborating with the English Electric Co in the design of two 1,600hp main-line locomotives. English Electric was one of the few British companies that had experience in the field, although as far as the LMS was concerned such experience had been confined to the world of the diesel shunter. The first LMS/EE locomotive, No 10000, emerged from Derby Works in December 1947. The Co-Co locomotive had cabs at each end of its bodywork, with two 'noses' that somewhat resembled

favoured American practice. The 16-cylinder engine was later used, in modified and increasingly more powerful form, in Class 40 and Class 50 designs.

The original SR order of 1946 did eventually translate into actual locomotives, but not until November 1950, when No 10201 emerged from Ashford Works, No 10202 following in August 1951. Both locomotives were designed jointly by O. V. S. Bulleid, SR Chief Mechanical Engineer, and C. M. Cook, SR Chief Electrical Engineer. Both locomotives also utilised the English Electric 16-cylinder 1,600hp power unit and had driving cabs at each end, but unlike the LMS examples neither had a protruding nose. The SR locomotives used a 1Co-Co1 wheel arrangement to help distribute their not inconsiderable weight of 135 tons gross, which placated the civil-engineering authorities! By the time these locomotives appeared the 16-cylinder EE engine had been developed to produce 1,750hp — a small contribution to the power-to-weight ratio, compared with the lighter but less powerful LMS locomotives. In March 1954 the third locomotive, No 10203, was built at Brighton Works. This incorporated a significant number of improvements based on the experience gained with earlier locomotives and the significant development of the EE 16SVT engine, now rated at 2,000hp, with a stepless pneumatic control system. A few tons were also shaved off the overall weight compared with the earlier sister machines, the locomotive turning the scales at 132 tons 16cwt.

The first revenue-earning run into Devon by an SR diesel occurred on 15 October 1951, when No 10202 worked the 1pm Waterloo–Plymouth/Ilfracombe as far as Exeter Central — the first instance of main-line diesel working in the county. (It should be mentioned that the unusual Brown-Boveri gas-turbine locomotive, No 18000, had worked to Plymouth in 1950 and that Metropolitan-Vickers gas-turbine No 18100 appeared in 1952, but although these looked like diesel locomotives they were in fact powered by other means.) Nos 10201/2 worked regularly into Devon, and although in 1952 both locomotives were despatched to Brighton Works for modifications and classified repairs, they returned to the former LSWR main line in the spring of 1953. Around the same time the two original LMS diesels, Nos 10000/1, were also allocated to Nine Elms and were

Built at Derby Railway Works in 1947 by the London, Midland & Scottish Railway were the first two main-line diesels with English Electric power units. Although used initially on former LMS lines they were transferred to the Southern Region (SR) of British Railways (BR) between 1953 and 1955, being allocated to Nine Elms depot in London. Like their later SR cousins they appeared regularly on trains from Waterloo to Exeter (and Bournemouth). No 10000 is seen passing Raynes Park with the down 'Bournemouth Belle' on 19 April 1953.
J. H. Aston / Author's collection

Although the three diesel-electric locomotives (Nos 10201-3) worked into Devon on the former LSWR main line between 1951 and 1955 they returned to works for modifications in 1952/3.
The diesels were also tried on the 'Bournemouth Belle' and the 'Golden Arrow' expresses, but no photographs have been discovered of the class working beyond Exeter. Sharing dirty depots with steam locomotives was not conducive to early diesel reliability, ash and grimy surroundings being scarcely compatible with complex electrical components. Here, on 20 August 1954, No 10202 shares Exmouth Junction shed with 'West Country' Pacific No 34024 *Tamar Valley. H. C. Casserley*

used extensively between Waterloo, Salisbury and Exeter. In 1954 there were only two diagrams for the diesels — the 9am and 1pm Waterloo–Exeter and 4.30pm and 5.53pm returns. The locomotives also headed such famous trains as the 'Bournemouth Belle', 'Golden Arrow' and 'Night Ferry', the last two on an experimental basis. The early diesels had to share accommodation with steam locomotives, and such dirty surroundings were hardly conducive to the intricacies of electrical control and transmission systems. During October 1954 dates had been set aside for testing the SR diesel-electrics between Exeter and Plymouth via the SR route and between Exeter and Barnstaple, but the trips were cancelled due to the non-availability of the locomotives, and it would appear that these early diesels never worked beyond Exeter. In early 1955 all but one of these locomotives were transferred away from the Southern to the London Midland Region (No 10203 finally joining its cousins on 20 July), where the SR machines would last until 1962/3. Between 1955 and 1958 main-line diesel traction was absent from the West Country, but this situation was soon to change dramatically.

In 1955 the British Transport Commission announced its Modernisation Plan, projected to cost £1,240 million — an absolute fortune in those now far-off days. The expenditure covered just about every aspect of railway operation, including signalling, the permanent way, electrification, 'dieselisation', coaching stock, freight-wagon stock, stations, marshalling and goods yards and a wide range of sundry items, but we are concerned here only with the procurement of diesel traction and the elimination of steam-locomotive building. The BTC stated that 'the steam locomotive's advantages of low first cost, simplicity, robustness and long life are now more than offset by the increase in all-round efficiency possible with other forms of traction, as evidenced in North America and Europe'. The demise was also justified by a lack of suitable coal and by the perpetual demand for a reduction in air pollution, which was significantly exacerbated by steam locomotives, and for greater cleanliness in trains and at railway stations. It was becoming more difficult to attract staff to the hard and dirty tasks of firing, cleaning and servicing steam locomotives. The BTC was also

looking for increases in locomotive performance, especially in acceleration — an area where the steam locomotive could simply not compete with diesel or electric traction. It recognised that, although the capital cost of a diesel locomotive was up to three times that of a steam locomotive of equal power, the former's availability figures were significantly superior.

The BTC stated that it did not intend to mix steam and diesel traction and that, as far as possible, it intended to turn whole areas over to exclusively diesel haulage. This policy would provide a useful and practical data-bank on the costs of diesel operation, which had not been possible 'with the tinkering that has gone on with the five engines so far in service' (see previous paragraphs). In 1955 it was intended that there would eventually be no fewer than 2,500 main-line diesel locomotives in service. At this stage only two areas in the whole of the UK were identified for total 'dieselisation' — the Western Region west of Newton Abbot and the Western Section main lines of the Southern Region, from Waterloo to Weymouth and Exeter. As far as Devon and Cornwall were concerned, the BTC stated that diesels would also work a large proportion of the passenger and freight trains between the South West and London/Bristol. There was also a plan for the extensive construction of diesel multiple-units and diesel shunters, for use in the South West (and elsewhere). All in all this policy would have substantial impact upon the area covered within this volume.

During the 1950s the BTC was faced with something of a dilemma in its intended conversion to diesel traction: should it adopt a 'big bang' approach, procuring large numbers of locomotives from the outset, or conduct trials with numerous different designs, in various power ranges and from a number of manufacturers, before placing bulk orders. It chose the latter course. In announcing the Modernisation Plan it stated that 'those [locomotives] at present in use on British Railways are of several types and to some extent of experimental design. Before final decisions are taken as to the types required for bulk delivery, a pilot scheme will be brought into operation under which extensive trials can be made.' Under the Pilot Scheme some 171 diesels would be procured, comprising 40 Type A locomotives (800-1,000hp), 106 Type B (1,000-1,200hp) and 25 Type C

(2,000hp and over). A provision was made that three Type A or B and two Type C locomotives should be able to work together in multiple. Only 11 locomotives of the initial 171 would be diesel-hydraulics, the remainder having electric transmission. There was a huge debate on whether, once the tendering process had been completed, the new locomotives should be built in the workshops of the successful private companies or in BR workshops. There were also political overtones in that British industry was still trying to recover after World War 2, and although there was little doubt that modified 'off the shelf' locomotives could have been procured from (particularly) the USA and Germany there was enormous pressure to support jobs and industry in the UK. As only 10% of the BR workshop workforce was employed on new-build locomotives it was presumed that giving the private companies construction work would not have a serious impact on BR staff numbers. Foreign companies were allowed a foot in the door: where such companies held licences to construct their particular products in the UK they could compete, for example in the provision of diesel engines and transmission systems; at the

time this applied particularly to Sulzer (Swiss), MAN and Voith (both German).

The power ranges were subsequently revised to become Type 1 (800-1,000hp), Type 2 (1,000-1,499hp), Type 3 (1,500-1,999hp), Type 4 (2,000-2,999hp) and Type 5 (3,000hp and over). The last category reflected the fact that during 1955, in a private venture, English Electric had put other designs in the shade by building its twin-engined prototype 'Deltic', which 106-ton locomotive produced no less than 3,300hp. (Perhaps indicative of a lack of direction with regard to the future of Britain's railways, its appearance was followed by BR's announcement that the Southern Region's Bulleid Pacific steam locomotives were to be extensively rebuilt!)

In November 1955 full details of the initial orders were released by the BTC. The list included such machines as the original 'Peaks' (later to become Class 44), the Metropolitan-Vickers Co-Bos (Class 28) and the original Brush/Mirrlees A1A-A1As (Class 30), but we are concerned here only with the Western Region. The only locomotives built specifically for the WR were from the North British Locomotive Co. These were the 11 diesel-hydraulic locomotives mentioned in the original plan and comprised five A1A-A1A twin-engined 2,000hp examples and six B-B 1,000hp machines. Both were to be fitted with Voith transmissions. It had been estimated that the 'dieselisation' of all trains west of Newton Abbot would require 130 locomotives, so other locomotive developments and orders had to run concurrently with the delivery of the first 11 machines. Having

On 12 February 1962 experimental Co-Co No D0280 (later D1200) *Falcon* worked from Swindon to Plymouth with a massive 550-ton test train that included a Dynamometer coach and is seen here approaching Teignmouth. The locomotive utilised two high-speed Maybach diesel engines, but unlike the Class 52s it had electric transmission. It worked on BR for 13 years before being withdrawn. *C. J. Marsden collection*

In 1955 BR announced its Modernisation Plan, costing £1,240 million — a vast sum in those now far-off days. Part of the plan envisaged the elimination of steam and the considerable expansion of both electric and diesel traction. BR conducted a Pilot Scheme to evaluate new locomotives and also planned to convert entire areas to diesel traction. One of the chosen areas was to the west of Newton Abbot, including large chunks of Devon and all of Cornwall. It was intended to experiment with both diesel-hydraulic locomotives, which had a proven track record in Germany, and diesel-electrics, much favoured in the USA. There were to be five twin-engined 2,000hp diesel-hydraulics built by the North British Locomotive Co. Shortly after being introduced in 1958 No D601 *Ark Royal* stands at the head of an up express at Penzance. *J. H. Aston*

completed trials in Scotland, No D600 was delivered to the WR towards the end of 1957 for driver training to take place, and by February 1958 it was heading its first revenue-earning train; by June 1958 No D601 was powering the down 'Cornish Riviera Express'. Also in 1958 some diesel shunters destined for the WR were being constructed, but the main news was the delivery of the first three 79-ton 2,000hp B-B 'Warships', ordered by the WR in 1956 as an adjunct to the Pilot Scheme (and bringing to 174 the total number of main-line diesels ordered).

On 19 March 1958 No D600 made its first visit to its eventual home base of Plymouth with a test train from Swindon, via Westbury. On 11 June No D601 was busy in Devon conducting double-heading trials with steam locomotives of the 'Castle', 'Hall' and 'Manor' 4-6-0 classes. In July Nos D600/1 both had fixed diagrams working into Cornwall. In the same month No D800, the first of the smaller 2,000hp (actual rating 2,070hp) 'Warships' was working on the WR, followed by Nos D801/2. These twin-Maybach-engined locomotives had Mekydro hydraulic transmission. The production Maybach-engined (Class 42) and NBL/MAN-engined (Class 43) 'Warships', Nos D803-70, would be rated at 2,200hp (actual rating 2,270hp and 2,200hp respectively), except for No D830, its two Paxman engines together being rated at 2,270hp.

By 1959 all of the original A1A-A1A 'Warships' had been delivered and were busy on a variety of duties including the prestigious Class 1 'Cornish Riviera' and 'Royal Duchy' expresses, in conjunction with the first batch of later 'Warships'. As an aside, No D804, heading the accelerated 'Bristolian' express on 15 June 1959, completed the 117.6 miles between London and Bristol in 100 minutes. By the end of 1959 locomotive deliveries had reached D813 and D6307. Over the South Devon banks steam and diesel locomotives were still sharing duties, and over the steepest climbs one of the small 'D63xx' diesels or sometimes a 'Warship' often piloted steam locomotives. On occasions express trains were double-headed in Devon and Cornwall by pairs of 'D63xx', but their 75mph speed limitation prevented their regular use beyond Exeter.

As already mentioned, maintenance of steam and diesel locomotives in the same depot had risks due to the possible contamination of electrical and mechanical components of the diesels by coal-dust, ash and the dirty surroundings which were associated with the steam locomotive. In the early days two roads of Plymouth Laira steam depot were dedicated to diesel locomotives, but eventually splendid new facilities were provided at Laira, Newton Abbot and Bristol Bath Road. Laira was formally opened in 1961. At other depots, especially the smaller sheds, diesels would have to co-habit with their steam counterparts between 1962 and 1965, while steam was being phased out.

By mid-1960 deliveries of new diesels had reached D822 and D6326, and by this time also North British-built MAN-engined 'Warships' were arriving to join the BR Swindon-built Maybach-engined versions. The 'Warships' worked in both Devon and Cornwall, but as numbers increased they could be found on many other WR routes, particularly from Paddington to Birmingham or Bristol. On 15 June 1961 No D7000, the first of 101 1,700hp (actual rating 1,740hp) 'Hymek' diesel-hydraulic locomotives (Class 35), was handed over to the WR. These locomotives were part of the plan to 'dieselise' the Bristol area and to supplement services west thereof. However, they turned their hand to a variety of duties, from humble freights to Swansea/Hereford–London expresses. The class later penetrated the West Country, and while they were never the most numerous type of locomotive to operate in Devon they were regular performers, Laira and Newton Abbot each having an allocation. In the meantime the 'Warships' and the 'D63xxs' appeared on other lines and branches in Devon and Cornwall. For example, on 2 September 1961 No D810 was noted at Crewkerne on the 8.15am Perranporth–Paddington, diverted via the LSWR main line because of a landslip at Westbury; at such times WR expresses were diverted via Okehampton, on the former LSWR main line.

The first main-line diesel-electrics to be allocated to the WR appeared in the autumn of 1961, when, to replace ex-LMS 'Jubilee' steam locomotives, some 2,500hp 'Peaks' (later Class 45) were transferred to Bristol Barrow Road shed. Although these lumbering 1Co-Co1s, weighing in at 136 tons, would work mainly the Birmingham road, it would be only a matter of time before they penetrated the true South West.

Completed in 1961, the first of the impressive and handsome

C-C 'Western' (Class 52) diesel-hydraulics was observed under-going trials on 13 January 1962. The Western Region recognised that in order for timetables to be universally accelerated it needed a 2,700hp locomotive and, although experiments would later be conducted with pairs of 'Warships' and Class 37s, considered a more powerful Type 4 locomotive a more viable option than double-heading with less powerful machinery. If a 'Hymek' was the equivalent of a 'Hall' 4-6-0 steam locomotive and a B-B 'Warship' equated to a 'Castle', then the 'Westerns' would be the WR's 'King' replacements. The 'Westerns' had two Maybach engines, each rated at 1,350hp (actual output 1,380hp), with Voith hydraulic transmission sets. By September 1962 the first seven 'Westerns' had all been allocated to Plymouth Laira.

Around this time the hybrid Co-Co No D0280 *Falcon* was working on the WR, from time to time finding its way into Devon. This locomotive, from the Brush Electrical Engineering Co, used 'Western'-type high-speed Maybach engines coupled to electric transmission. In August 1962 another prototype, No D0260 *Lion* (a product of the Birmingham Railway Carriage & Wagon Co, Sulzer and AEI), was tested over the South Devon banks. Other notable events of 1962 were the completion of the rebuilt Plymouth North Road station — after six years of effort!

— and a temporary reduction in the maximum speed of the 'Warships' to 80mph, due to ride problems caused partly by excessive wheel-flange wear.

In March 1963 the Western Region received its first English Electric Type 3s (Class 37), this 1,750hp Co-Co design having been introduced on the Eastern Region in 1960. Initially the WR's examples would all be allocated to South Wales, and it would be some time before they became part of the traction scene in Devon and Cornwall, but in due course the class would beat all records in terms of diesel-locomotive availability. Later in 1963 the WR received its first allocation of the versatile Brush/Sulzer Type 4, the first two (Nos D1682/3) arriving at Old Oak Common on 31 October (although it would be 1965 before the new OOC diesel facility was completed). Initially these 2,750hp Co-Cos (later derated to 2,580hp and to become better known as Class 47s) replaced 'Western' diesel-hydraulics on the Paddington–Birmingham route, although they would appear regularly in Devon and Cornwall from 1967, notably on the 'Clayfreighter' diagram.

From 1963 most branch-line services were gradually taken over by new diesel multiple-units, but in some cases 'D63xx' diesels replaced steam locomotives, albeit still hauling steam-age rolling stock. However, in 1964 DMUs continued to work some Cornish local services, including the 12.00 Penzance–Plymouth. Meanwhile a small four-wheeled railbus was working Bodmin North–Wadebridge services in Cornwall, but such services were short-lived. Gardner-engined 0-6-0 diesel shunters (Class 03) were working the Wenford goods (having replaced steam tank locomotives) and saw use on other minor freight lines, especially in the Plymouth area. All classes of diesel-hydraulic locomotive were working throughout the WR but particularly in Devon and Cornwall, where they headed most classes of train, from humble freight to top-link express. A major development occurred on

No D600 ('D' for 'Diesel') was delivered to the WR after running trials in Scotland at the end of 1957, first being used on a revenue-earning train in February 1958. These 117-ton A1A-A1A locomotives had a maximum service speed of 90mph, and each carried steam-heating equipment to heat rolling stock. The locomotives were later designated Class 41. They were soon put to work on the most prestigious express trains such as the 'Cornish Riviera', seen here approaching Newton Abbot in October 1959 behind No D602 *Bulldog*. *Ian Allan Library*

7 September, when B-B 'Warships' took over the Waterloo–Exeter services from Southern Region steam locomotives (by then in terminal decline), a successful trial having been conducted on 26 August.

From 14 June 1965 there were further significant improvements in the West Country timetable, Paddington–Exeter journey times being reduced to 153 minutes for the 174 miles and Torquay (198 miles) being reached in 200 minutes, the first stop being Dawlish! On 3 June 1965 a pair of Class 37s, Nos D6881/2, were involved in some high-speed trials. Working in multiple, the 3,500hp combination set WR rails alight by travelling from Paddington to Taunton in 107 minutes 25 seconds (at that time an absolute record), Exeter in 132 minutes 21 seconds and Plymouth in 196 minutes 17 seconds — all with 10 coaches (350 tons) in tow! On another test Bristol–Paddington was reeled off in a remarkable 86 minutes 35 seconds.

From the latter part of 1965 the B-B 'Warships' were outshopped in maroon livery, Nos D813/57/8/60/2/3/5/70 being noted. However, from June 1966 the standard 'Rail Blue' was adopted, and gradually the greens and maroons disappeared; meanwhile small yellow warning panels gave way to full yellow front ends, all in the interests of visibility and safety. On 15 June A1A-A1A 'Warship' No D600 was noted at Truro in all-blue livery and with dual route-indicator boxes on each side of each nose end, the latter modification having first been applied to No D603 on overhaul at Swindon Works late in 1965. In October 1966 it was announced that all five of these original 'Warships' would be transferred to South Wales to work coal trains, but only two months later, in a surprise move, it was decided that they would be withdrawn, after a lifespan of less than 10 years. It would be September 1968 before Nos D600/1 were hauled from Laira to Woodham's yard at Barry for scrapping (although No D601 would linger until 1980!), the other three locomotives meeting a similar fate at Cashmore's of Newport, South Wales. By contrast the B-B 'Warships' of Classes 42 and 43, despite by now having up to a million miles on the clock and being regarded by BR as non-standard (as explained in the following paragraphs), were surprisingly selected to work in multiple (with the aid of special 36-wire connectors) to speed up the West Country timetables still further. Working again at their 90mph maximum speed, Class 42s in pairs were scheduled to travel from Paddington to Plymouth in just 225 minutes, including stops at Taunton and Exeter. When a pair of 'Warships' was not available a single Class 52 'Western' was used, incurring a modest time loss.

From October 1968 the 'D' was dropped from diesel-locomotive numbers, because all steam locomotives on BR had been withdrawn and there was no longer any need for a distinction. Although renumbered 'on paper' the majority of the 'Westerns' were not physically modified because their numbers took the form of plates cast in alloy, and the 'D' could not easily be removed. From the same year brake vans were no longer required on fully fitted freight trains.

In the autumn of 1968, as part of the implementation of its National Traction Plan (produced in 1965), BR announced that 28 classes of main-line diesel locomotive were to be reduced to just 15, and this led to the almost immediate demise of the already-vulnerable Clayton Type 1s and Metropolitan-Vickers and English Electric Type 2s. Also vulnerable were the NBL Type 2s and in due course all of the B-B 'Warships', diesel-hydraulic types now being considered non-standard; by 19 October Type 2s Nos D6300/2-5/13 were all in South Wales for scrapping, while 'Warships' Nos D800-2 had been withdrawn

between August and October. However, a truly remarkable performance occurred on 5 May 1969, when, despite nearing their 'sell by' date, Nos D819/08 set a record with the down 'Cornish Riviera' (which had once again become 'Limited', with just an eight-coach load), reaching Exeter St Davids in just 131 minutes 30 seconds (schedule 139 minutes), at an average speed of 80mph, and Plymouth in 203 minutes (seven minutes early on the new 3½-hour timing), averaging 70mph overall. On the downside, in November 1969 the WR reduced maintenance expenditure by eliminating *all* main-works overhauls for the generally inferior NBL-built Class 43 'Warships'.

With the decision to standardise on diesel-electric types the WR now began to receive classes hitherto associated with other regions, including Brush Type 2s (Class 31), of which No 5533 was noted at Old Oak Common in October 1968. By 1969 pairs of SR Class 33 1,550hp 'Cromptons' were regularly working the 08.50 Brighton–Exeter St Davids on Saturdays, while the 08.02 from Waterloo was also sometimes 'Crompton'-worked, and in March 1970 two pairs of Class 33s worked into Cornwall for the first time with London–St Germans Chartex specials. Meanwhile, on 5 January 1969, Class 45 'Peak' No 28 had been 'unusually' noted at Plymouth — a precursor of things to come; from 7 October 1969 'Peaks' regularly worked the 'Devonian' through from Bristol to Paignton, and on 30 December a Class 46 worked into Cornwall, returning with the 16.20 ex-Penzance. In early January 1970 several of the class were noted in the Plymouth area; by now Class 45s, 46s and 47s were all regular — indeed, daily — visitors to Devon and Cornwall, and Laira would later receive an allocation of Class 46s.

With the influx of diesel-electrics large numbers of 'Warships' were now being placed in store, but the latter remained regular performers in the South West, while in July 1970 Class 22 No D6333 was still busy working milk trains to Torrington.

A particularly black day for hydraulic fans was 22 May 1971, when 15 'Warships' and 15 '63xx' Class 22 locomotives were withdrawn. On 30 July 1971 Class 25 No 5180, newly transferred from the London Midland Region, was noted at Laira on a freight working. The Class 25s had arrived to replace the last of the NBL Class 22s; No 5180 arriving at Laira in July. In November 1971 some 29 different 'Peaks' were noted in the South West in a five-day period! Another significant change occurred from 4 October 1971, when, after a reign of seven years, Class 42s were replaced on Waterloo–Exeter workings by Class 33s. However, 'Warships' were still trusted sufficiently to undertake Royal Train duties, No D818 being so employed from Exeter to Barnstaple on 10 November 1971.

The last of the Class 22s was withdrawn at the beginning of 1972, although some, withdrawn in 1968, had had a life of only six years! In the summer of 1972 a number of Class 42s were reinstated due to a general shortage of motive power. 'Hymeks' too were still active, and on 1 July No D7029 worked the 08.15 Paddington–Barnstaple. Changes in the motive-power scene continued in October, when Class 31 No 5632 worked the 06.30 Plymouth–Paddington parcels. In December the last of the surviving 'Warships' was withdrawn from service, although No 832 worked to Derby Technical Centre under its own power on 10 January 1973. Also in January 1973 'Westerns' Nos D1023 and D1058 became the last Class 52 'Westerns' to receive a heavy works overhaul; it was the beginning of the end for this famous class. On 17 March 1973 every single main-line express in Cornwall was Class 52-hauled, but during May the first of the class was formally withdrawn. However, the reality was that many of the class had already been cannibalised at Laira for spare parts and were classified as stored unserviceable! In October the new BR 'TOPS' (Total Operations Processing System) computer system was introduced, which would result in the renumbering of all locomotives (except the Class 52s), whereby the new locomotive number began with the class number. By now all the surviving 'Hymeks' were based in the London area, but on 11 December No 7093 worked the Chard–Exeter milk train. On 31 August 1974 the same locomotive unusually worked the 15.55 Exeter–Barnstaple and 17.55 return, but by March 1975 the last of the class had been withdrawn.

By 10 November 1973 the first of the Class 50s to be transferred from the London Midland Region had arrived at Laira for crew training, and this was to be the start of a long association between these 2,700hp English Electric locomotives and the counties of Devon and Cornwall. The last express passenger diesel locomotives built for BR, the Class 50s were capable of 100mph running and had the added advantages of air brakes and electric train-heating facilities. All of the class would eventually be transferred from the London Midland to the Western Region, replacing the much-loved Class 52 'Westerns'. However, as late as May 1975 a 'Western' was timed by a reputable train-timer at 102mph; such was the type's unrealised potential. In January 1976 BR headcodes on locomotives were abolished, and until indicator panels were 'blanked-off' many locomotives ran with '0000' showing as a train identifier; the 'Westerns', however, tended to display the locomotive number. The class soldiered on until February 1977, and the author had the privilege of running the last farewell specials, from Paddington to Meldon Quarry in October 1976 and to three Cornish branch lines in December 1976; although one of the class was noted at Penzance later in the month, this effectively marked the end of the 19-year diesel-hydraulic era in the South West.

By 1979 it was the turn of diesel-electric classes to feel the pinch, when Class 37s arrived in Devon and Cornwall to replace the somewhat underpowered Class 25s. Although there would still be a handful of locomotive-hauled passenger trains in Devon and Cornwall in 2004 the 'rot' started as long ago as September 1979, when the prestigious 'Cornish Riviera' and 'Golden Hind' expresses were converted to operation by IC125 units. First introduced to the WR in 1976 on services between Paddington and Bristol/South Wales, these represented a new era in passenger comfort and demolished every standing record in terms of journey time. Even over the South Devon banks and on the switchback Cornish main line they performed admirably, and with 4,500hp available so they should have!

From May 1980 Class 50s ousted the small but purposeful Class 33 'Cromptons' from the Waterloo–Exeter St Davids route, increasing their extensive geographical coverage. Beginning in 1979, the Class 50s received extensive refurbishment (a process completed in 1983), and from 1980 they started to appear in a new 'large logo' livery with wrap-around yellow ends; this was later extended to other classes, providing some relief from the drab all-over blue. In December 1980 the axe finally fell on the WR Class 46s, and accordingly Laira lost its allocation. These locomotives had worked passenger and freight trains throughout the South West but were arguably best known for their long freight hauls to Stoke-on-Trent and Carlisle.

The early 1980s represented a period of relative stability in terms of motive power. In 1981 trials were conducted on the Gunnislake branch with a Class 140 railbus, while with effect from the 1982 summer timetable fewer IC125 units worked through to Penzance, resulting in an increase in local locomotive-hauled trains in Cornwall. From October 1985 Class 45 'Peaks' were banned west of Bristol, bringing to an end the era of the 16-wheeled locomotives in Devon and Cornwall. There would, of course, be many other changes on the locomotive front, but these occurred outside the timespan covered by this book.

*   *   *

In addition to line closures and the long and varied story on the motive-power scene there were many other changes in the 1951-85 'Diesel Days' period. The entire railway infrastructure changed tremendously. The most visible change towards the end of the period covered in this volume involved signalling. The replacement of semaphore signalling crept like a cancer down from Paddington as, section by section, colour lights replaced their lower-quadrant predecessors. With the replacement of signals came the abolition of signalboxes, of which those at Exeter St Davids and Newton Abbot were particularly impressive examples. At larger stations there were usually signalboxes at each end of station sites, giving the enthusiast some warning of imminent train arrivals and departures. There had been some pockets of colour-light signalling in the earlier days, particularly around Plymouth, but eventually it was only in the county of Cornwall that the old-fashioned semaphore signalling survived. Although much rationalised, manual signalling still endures in the Royal Duchy.

Other changes have included track rationalisation, encompassing entire branch lines, goods yards, depots and even stretches of main line. Parts of the former LSWR main line east of Pinhoe, the eastern approaches to the Royal Albert Bridge and the line between Burngullow and Probus in Cornwall were singled (although in 2004 the last was being reinstated!). The freight scene changed hugely, and the disappearance of wagonload freight and the pick-up goods, plus the general downturn in freight by rail, has transformed the scene. Coaching stock has also changed, vacuum-braked Mk 1 stock giving way firstly to Mk 2 dual-braked / dual-heated stock and later to Mk 2d/e air-braked, air-conditioned and electrically heated stock. Eventually the majority of main-line expresses and local passenger workings would comprise multiple-units of various descriptions, but in this volume only the venerable first-generation diesel-mechanical units and the earlier days of HST units are featured.

It should be pointed out at this stage that the braking and heating capabilities of the various locomotives and rolling stock was something of a nightmare for the railway operators. Some early diesel locomotives had only vacuum brakes and some were dual-braked. The same applied to passenger rolling stock, but upon arrival of air-conditioned coaches only air brakes were the order of the day. Obviously the operators could not roster a vacuum-only-braked Class 52 to haul stock that was only air-braked. Many such locomotives were later converted to dual-braked status, while in other cases vacuum-only braking was used as an excuse to scrap locomotives. The same situation applied to goods wagons and freight stock. Train heating was also a problem, because some freight locomotives had no train-heating capability; some diesels had steam boilers on board to provide steam heating to coaches, while later arrivals were fitted only with electric train heating. Although the situation eased in the summer months, when non-boilered engines often worked passenger trains, in the winter months the operators had to be well aware, prior to diagramming, of each locomotive's braking and heating capabilities.

In 1983 an experiment was conducted whereby certain railway

operations in Cornwall were delegated to local management, based at St Blazey. The 'Cornish Railways' management were charged with certain financial and operational responsibilities and even had their own logo. Marketing was an important part of their remit, various railcards and rovers being available for travel as far as Plymouth, and in many ways this was a precursor of sectorisation. In 1986 the Cornish Railways experiment ceased, and few could then have realised that, long-term, the situation would become even more complex with the end of British Railways and the arrival of privatisation, with numerous train operators, wagon- and carriage-leasing companies and separate infrastructure ownership. Fortunately *Diesel Days: Devon and Cornwall* restricts itself to the period prior to these radical organisational changes!

One of the most remarkable changes between the steam and diesel eras concerned the versatility and availability of the diesels. Although there were mixed-traffic steam locomotives, the diesel demonstrated the quite remarkable ability to work a china-clay trip-freight working one day and head the 'Cornish Riviera' the next. Also the performance of the diesels, especially in terms of hill-climbing capability, was incomparable with the age of steam. For example, a 'Castle' could take a trailing load of only 315 tons over the South Devon banks unaided, and a 'King' was restricted to 360 tons. By comparison a Class 47 or 50 is permitted to travel from Newton Abbot to Plymouth unaided with no less than 580 tons in tow! In the days of steam a second engine was often added 'to the point' of a train, and in the late 1950s a single diesel was often used to pilot a steam locomotive over the banks. However, once steam finally disappeared in 1964 double-heading was normally seen only on the heaviest freight trains, in which case pairs of Class 25s (and, later, Class 37s) were used to attack the climbs of up to 1 in 37.

Compared with the late 1960s and the 1970s, the early days of the diesel era were very colourful, locomotives being painted

In 1956 an order had been placed for three lightweight 2,000/2,200hp B-B diesel-hydraulic locomotives. Turning the scales at just 79 tons, these twin-engined machines were between 38 and 54 tons lighter than diesel-electric locomotives with the same nominal power output. Built at Swindon Works, No D800 *Sir Brian Robertson*, with special headboard reading 'FIRST 2,200HP DIESEL HYDRAULIC LOCOMOTIVE', was photographed in July 1958 leaving Newton Abbot with a Penzance–Paddington express. Commonly known (like the earlier NBL machines) as 'Warships', these locomotives were later designated Class 42. *A. Windrush*

variously black, green, maroon or blue, or even 'desert sand' or 'golden ochre'. However a considerable degree of regional autonomy was lost as the corporate blue was universally adopted. When dirty— not uncommon at this time — the livery became very drab and was not really conducive to dull-weather monochrome railway photography, and 'one-off' paint jobs and the advent of the 'large logo' livery in 1980 represented the only rays of sunshine in a rather monotonous period of locomotive liveries. In the early days there was some variety in rolling-stock livery, with maroon, 'blood and custard' and brown-and-cream coaches appearing, but, as mentioned earlier, for much of the time it was grey-and-blue for main-line stock and all-blue for local and suburban stock. Freight wagons offered more variety, especially the privately owned examples.

As mentioned in the Introduction, it is difficult to identify the optimum period of 'diesel days' in Devon and Cornwall from the enthusiasts' perspective. Arguably the years 1965/6 or 1976/7 would be optimum, the former because these were the years immediately following the end of steam, when all trains were powered by diesel engines and when diesel-hydraulics ruled, the latter because there was still a mix of diesel-electric and diesel-hydraulic locomotives at a time when IC125 units and their

successors had not yet arrived and when locomotive-hauled stock and a variety of freight flows could still be seen. Another alternative for some would be 1980, when main-line trains were Class 45-, 47- or 50-hauled, HSTs appearing only on named trains, and when the impressive Class 37s were arriving in significant numbers to oust the few remaining Class 25s. The Class 37s have since enjoyed a 20-year career in the South West — longer than any of the diesel-hydraulic classes. With increasing standardisation it will probably be the General Motors Class 66s that eventually gain the longevity crown, which is currently held by the venerable Class 47s in their many guises, with over 37 years of service in Devon and Cornwall.

To summarise and in retrospect this book illustrates what can only be called modern-traction nostalgia. There is probably not a single one of the 290 photographs in this collection that could now be repeated. All those who experienced the first decade of diesel traction no doubt find it hard to believe that over 45 years have now elapsed since the first 'Warship' arrived in the West Country and that well over a quarter of a century has passed since the 'Westerns' were withdrawn. It is even a quarter of a century since the IC125 High Speed Train units first crossed the River Tamar from Devon to Cornwall. Many classes have come and gone, some types have been preserved, while others have been consigned to oblivion except for photographic evidence, as featured within. Rolling stock and goods wagons have also changed significantly. Old unbraked or vacuum-braked four-

Another class of WR locomotive arising from the Modernisation Plan and ordered at the same time as the North British A1A-A1As was the 'D63xx' class, which later became Class 22. These small 65-ton B-B locomotives used NBL-assembled MAN engines, the six prototypes having these set at 1,000hp and later examples 1,100hp. The initial batch was for six locomotives numbered D6300-5, but before these were delivered a further order for 52 additional locomotives was placed. Shortly after delivery to the WR at the end of 1958 No D6301 leaves Exeter St Davids for Central station. *M. Dart collection*

wheeled wagons, including box vans and clay hoods, have disappeared, and modern air-braked wagons, running on axles with roller bearings and disc brakes, have replaced them. One or two excursion sets aside, the age of the Mk 1 coach has long since passed, and even Mk 2 varieties are all but extinct. Numerous lines have been closed and the tracks ripped up, with new post-closure private and commercial buildings preventing their ever reopening. These lines are relegated to the annals of history and survive only in pictures, books and on film. In places the railway infrastructure has changed out of all recognition. Many stations have closed, surviving stations have been rebuilt, goods sheds have been demolished, signalboxes abandoned, track rationalised, signs changed, lamp standards upgraded etc, but on the positive side these features are all recorded for posterity in *Diesel Days: Devon and Cornwall*, which provides the opportunity to view a modern era that is already history. Enjoy the railtour!

Above: Just passing into Devon from Cornwall with a delightfully mixed engineer's special on Sunday 29 April 1962 is NBL/MAN Type 2 diesel-hydraulic (later Class 22) No D6312. From the single track over the Royal Albert Bridge the train is entering double track. The road bridge across the River Tamar in the background was then brand-new. In later years the single-line section would be extended further east and the signalbox and semaphore signals abolished. *Brian Haresnape*

Below: The NBL Type 2 diesel-hydraulics cost about £65,000 each in 1958 values. The last of the 58 locomotives (the full quota of the Type 2 power range envisaged for the South West) was not delivered until February 1962. This explains the almost new paintwork on No D6353, double-heading an earlier sister locomotive on a down express at Newton Abbot on 28 July 1962. *R. P. Crane*

Top left: Few could argue that the NBL Type 2s were a success, the locomotives' maximum output of 1,100hp meaning that in the hilly West Country all heavy passenger and freight trains had to be double-headed. It took a considerable time to integrate with steam infrastructure, and in the early days, at the time the locomotives were delivered, the new and purpose-built depots at Newton Abbot and Plymouth Laira were not ready for service. However, the locomotives were unreliable, and by 1967 withdrawals had begun. The survivors were eventually repainted from green into corporate 'Rail blue', in which livery No 6356 (the 'D' having been dispensed with) was toying with some parcels vans at Newton Abbot on 2 August 1971. *David Wharton*

Top right: NBL Type 2s were at home either on light freight trains or on short local passenger trains and were regular performers on Devon and Cornwall branch lines. Heading a two-coach local (Bodmin– Padstow) Class 2 train is No D6341, seen approaching Wadebridge. The signals on the left control trains on the Halwill Junction-Wadebridge line. Passenger services through Wadebridge ceased in January 1967. The trackbed now forms part of the Camel Trail footpath/ cycleway. *Mike Daly / Murice Dart collection*

Lower left: When photographed on 13 July 1971 No 6338 was one of the last 10 survivors of the class. The design featured old-fashioned-looking spoke wheels with a diameter of 43in, which were dynamically balanced, while Nos D6334-57 were fitted from new with twin headcode boxes with two roller blinds in each; code 7B45 seen here designates a Class 7 freight working. No 6338 stands in the long since abandoned up Liskeard goods yard with a rake of box vans. Note the china-clay empties on the left. *G. F. Gillham*

Lower right: Passenger trains between Newton Abbot and Moretonhampstead ceased back in March 1959, but aside from short periods of closure the branch has continued in operation ever since as a freight-only line as far as Heathfield. Here, on 15 July 1971, the daily freight from Heathfield approaches Newton Abbot behind No 6308. The headcode boxes were added during works overhaul. Delivered in January 1960, the locomotive would be withdrawn in September 1971, just eight weeks after this photograph was taken. *G. F. Gillham*

Above: Double-heading over the South Devon banks had been commonplace in the days of steam, so during the period of transition to diesel traction there were inevitably instances of trains being double-headed by a combination of steam and diesel locomotives. Having just breasted the climb, NBL/MAN Type 2 No D6330 and 'Hall' 4-6-0 No 6963 *Throwley Hall* emerge from Dainton Tunnel with a down train on 19 August 1961. *M. Pope*

Below: Original A1A-A1A 'Warship' No D602 *Bulldog* has just left the Falmouth branch and Highertown Tunnel at Truro with the 9.30am Falmouth–Paddington on 21 September 1959. Photographs of the class actually on the branch are rare. The train is passing the steam depot at Truro (83F), and on shed are a good selection of GWR 4-6-0s, including a very clean 'County', No 1008 *County of Cardigan*. *P. Q. Treloar*

Top left: This scene on the approach to Dainton Tunnel is dated not only by the telegraph posts but also by a green-liveried NBL/MAN Type 2 with steam-age headcode discs and no yellow warning panel. Displaying the express passenger code on 22 August 1959 is No D6305, one of the original batch of locomotives, coupled to 'Hall' No 5931 *Hatherley Hall* with an up train. *M. Dart collection*

Lower left: Although new diesel locomotives should not emit much exhaust, in this photograph 'Castle' 4-6-0 No 5058 *Earl of Clancarty* looks to be doing all the work and pushing North British Type 2 No D6317. The pair are leaving Newquay and approaching Tolcarne Junction with the 11.15 departure for Wolverhampton on Saturday 15 July 1961. *R. S. Clare*

Below: To steam enthusiasts the new diesels were 'boxes on wheels', and while that may be a little harsh there is no doubt, in this fine view at Aller Junction, west of Newton Abbot, that 'Castle' No 7037 *Swindon* looks more aesthetically pleasing than does its pilot locomotive, No D6336. The pair are heading for Penzance with the 5.30am from Paddington on 29 September 1961. *W. L. Underhay*

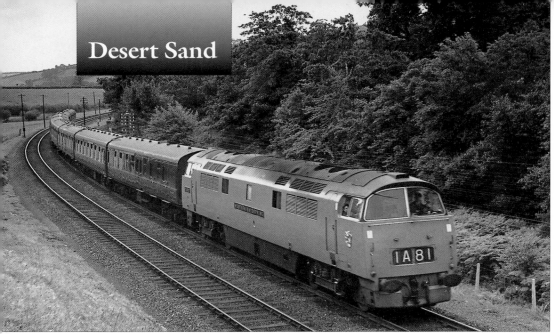

Desert Sand

If the 1,700hp 'Hymek' was the equivalent of a 'Hall' steam locomotive and the 2,200hp B-B 'Warship' was the equivalent of a 'Castle', then the 2,700hp twin-engined 'Western' was the equivalent of a 'King'. The extremely attractive 'Westerns' were introduced to improve schedules for the heaviest express trains on the WR. The first example, No D1000 *Western Enterprise,* emerged from works at the end of 1961 and was undergoing trials by January 1962. In its unique 'desert sand' livery the locomotive was photographed near Lostwithiel with train 1A81 — the up 'Cornish Riviera Express' — on 31 July 1962. *D. Ian Wood*

At the time of 'dieselisation' there were plenty of other changes being made to the railway infrastructure, one of the major projects being the complete rebuilding of Plymouth North Road station and the resignalling of the entire area, the project taking more than six years to complete! Posing in front of a part-finished North Road signalbox on 30 April 1962 is No D1000 *Western Enterprise;* note the alloy BR 'lion and wheel' emblem below the cab window. These locomotives would be regular visitors to the West Country for the next 15 years, although this particular example would be withdrawn as early as February 1974 — a life of little more than 12 years. *Brian Haresnape*

Depot Transformation

Above: The first of two photographs which serve to illustrate the dramatic difference in depot facilities afforded the new diesels in the early days of 'dieselisation'. For up to three years the shiny new machinery had to survive in the grimy surroundings associated with the steam locomotive. At Plymouth Laira two of the old steam roads were used by the diesels before the sheer weight of numbers necessitated using more of the old depot. The conditions are readily apparent in this view, recorded during a shed 'bash' in 1959. *M. Dart collection*

Below : Showing a marked contrast from the view above, this photograph depicts the brand-new diesel depot at Laira which was finally opened in 1962. The purpose-built structure enabled the new diesels to be stabled, maintained and cleaned in almost sterile surroundings. As an A1A-A1A 'Warship' (right) is cleaned the scene from left to right shows redundant steam locomotives, an English Electric 0-6-0 shunter (just visible), a B-B 'Warship', single- and twin-car DMUs, a 'Western', a 'D63xx', further B-B 'Warships' and (far right) a 204hp diesel-mechanical shunter. The depot remains in use more than 40 years later. *C. J. Marsden collection*

Maroon 'Westerns'

Over the years the 'Westerns' (later known as Class 52s) appeared in many liveries, including desert sand, green, maroon, golden ochre and various shades of blue, with numerous detailed variations. When clean the maroon looked very striking, but on 6 June 1970 No D1042 *Western Princess* had extremely tatty paintwork as it paused at Truro, Cornwall's county town, with the 10.00 Penzance–Bradford Exchange. This platform is no longer in use.
R. F. Roberts / Stephenson Locomotive Society

Below: A photograph showing the aesthetically pleasing lines of the ultimate WR-influenced design of diesel-hydraulic locomotive, the 2,700hp 'Western'. No D1046 *Western Marquis* passes between Kingskerswell and Aller Junction with the 10.45 Paignton–Paddington on 15 May 1969. In its National Traction Plan BR confirmed its intention to standardise on diesel-electric locomotives, and shortly after this photograph was taken maintenance schedules on Class 22s and Class 42s/43s were reduced, although this would not yet extend to the 'Westerns'.
Stephenson Locomotive Society

Above: Bound for the Midlands, 12 maroon Mk 1 coaches sweep along the sea wall just east of Teignmouth behind a gleaming maroon 'Western' sporting a small yellow warning panel. Designated 'Type 4' in power range, the design featured two high-revving 1,350hp Maybach diesel engines coupled to Voith hydraulic transmission sets. With a maximum service speed of 90mph these locomotives would be entrusted with heavy express trains throughout the 1962-77 period. *Ian Allan Library*

Below: It would be great to be aboard train 1A80, the 15.20 Penzance–Paddington, on a sunny 12 June 1969, as No D1002 *Western Explorer* negotiates Aller Junction, where the Plymouth and Paignton lines once formed a physical connection. Nowadays the location is called 'Aller Divergence', because the two lines now run independently into Newton Abbot, there being no actual 'junction' at Aller. *L. Riley*

Truro Goods Yard

Back in 1981 Truro still had a thriving goods yard. Over the years it has handled a wide range of freight, including coal; more recent examples have included fertiliser, explosives, calcified seaweed and even beer! In July of 1981 two young ladies, who will now be in their late 20s, observe Class 37 No 37 207 shunting the yard. The Class 37s arrived in Cornwall during 1979 to replace Class 25s, which in turn had replaced Class 22s! *Author*

It was always fascinating to see a 2,700hp express passenger locomotive on menial freight duties, and the West Country often obliged. Although this photograph was taken as recently as 1981 scenes such as this, complete with four-wheeled coal wagons, box vans, bogie flats and even a brake van, have long since vanished from our railways. Most of these wagons were vacuum-braked, and the locomotives working them had to be similarly equipped. No 50 029 *Renown* catches the early-morning light as its driver chats to the shunter, possibly about shunting manœuvres. *Author*

The 1,250hp Class 25s arrived in the West in July 1971 to replace the unsuccessful Class 22s. Leaving Truro yard on 28 July 1975 is No 25 223 with an up freight. The train had originated at St Erth, hence the two 3,000gal milk tankers behind the locomotive. All of the lines to the right in this view of Truro (East) signalbox, including the line being used here, have now been lifted, although the signalbox and semaphore signalling survive. *Brian Morrison*

Early DMUs

Diesel multiple-units (DMUs) had been a great success when introduced to Yorkshire in the mid-1950s, and the Modernisation Plan envisaged a substantial building programme so that the various types of unit could be used nationwide. Although there had been occasional visits to the South West in the late 1950s, new units started arriving in some numbers from 1960/1. In this fascinating view from 1960 a gleaming Birmingham Railway Carriage & Wagon Co (BRCW) unit (later Class 118), with coach W51326 visible, shares the grimy Truro steam shed with a collection of ex-GWR steam locomotives. *S. C. Nash*

The arrival of the three-car DMUs in the West Country sounded the death-knell for steam on local services in the Exeter area and represented a major step in the total conversion to diesel traction. Its green livery enhanced by cream 'whiskers' on its driving end, coach No W51318 leads a trio of three-car units at Exeter St Davids on 26 July 1960. These units were popular in that they were clean and soot-free, and the lucky passengers in the front seats had a wonderful view of the track ahead, unless an unfriendly driver lowered his blind! *Frank Church*

This splendid photograph, which encapsulates the atmosphere of the new diesel age, shows an absolutely gleaming ex-works BRCW three-car unit on a driver-training run passing Teignmouth on the up line on 4 June 1960. Note the lining or 'waistband', the revised 'lion and wheel' crest and the then novel headcode blind. *Les Elsey*

For use on very lightly used branch lines AC Cars Ltd built five 150hp four-wheeled railbuses. These weighed a mere 11 tons, with a commensurately light axle load. With seating for 46, they were tested on the WR from February 1958, and the travels of No W79977 included Newquay in Cornwall, seen here. Although they were to work in Cornwall many years later (see next photograph) the railbuses never took up residence on the Newquay line. *Author's collection*

From June 1964 the small AC railbuses were drafted into Cornwall to work a shuttle service from Bodmin North to Boscarne Junction, introduced as an economy measure to save costs and possibly (however unlikely) the line, a small wooden interchange platform having been built at Boscarne Junction so that railbus workings could connect with the Bodmin Road–Bodmin General–Wadebridge–Padstow services. On 24 July 1964 a railbus for Boscarne is seen at the buffer-stops at the now abandoned LSWR/SR terminus of Bodmin North. In 1965 a couple of railbus services would serve Bodmin General and Bodmin Road. *J. H. Aston/M. Dart collection*

Although far removed from the long line of illustrious steam locomotives the 'Cross-Country' DMUs (later Class 120) were nevertheless products of Swindon Works, being built between 1957 and 1960, and it was inevitable that they would find themselves working in the West Country. When photographed on 3 May 1959 these two units were forming a special excursion to Torquay and Paignton. With 1,200hp available from eight 150hp engines (two per driving car) the train is passing Shaldon Bridge, just west of Teignmouth. *David Sellman*

Dainton

Of all the South Devon banks Dainton is the most famous. For years trains have been grinding up the 1-in-36/38 gradient on either side of the tunnel, the heaviest being double-headed until the advent of the 2,500hp diesel locomotive. Passing a splendid wooden lower-quadrant semaphore signal, green NBL Type 2 No D6312 and green B-B 'Warship' No D868 *Zephyr* power 13 coaches towards the summit on 19 August 1961. *M. Pope*

Right: One can almost hear the booming from the four exhaust ports of the 2,700hp English Electric Class 50 blasting up the gradient and into Dainton Tunnel with an up train on 10 June 1978. The stock comprises air-conditioned coaches, except for the buffet car (second coach). Note that the old signalbox has been replaced by an ugly modern example and that the wooden signals have given way to the standard WR metal type. *Author*

Left: Not a yellow warning panel in sight as 'Warship' No D815 *Druid* passes Dainton Summit at about 28mph with the 5.30am Paddington–Plymouth express on 1 June 1960. Curiously the fourth coach of this Mk 1 rake is a suburban compartment coach with full-length running board! Refuge sidings can be seen on the right. *Les Elsey*

'Hymeks'

Left: The first of 101 'Hymek' Type 3s (later known collectively as Class 35) emerged from the works of Beyer Peacock at Gorton, Manchester, in April 1961. These purposeful 1,700hp locomotives were more than mere visitors in the South West, Newton Abbot and Laira (Plymouth) each having a small allocation, and although less numerous in the area than other WR diesel-hydraulic classes they were nevertheless regular performers. Photographed on 13 June 1964 approaching Mutley Tunnel, Plymouth, with a train for Plymouth Friary, No D7068 had travelled over the SR route from Exeter via Okehampton. *Maurice Dart*

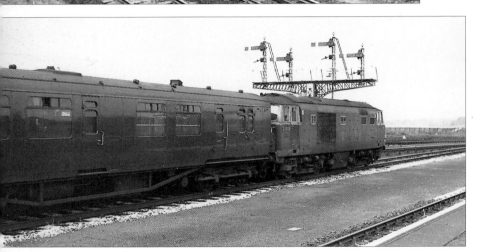

Left: Another shot with SR links is this rare view of No D7069 at Exmouth on Saturday 2 April 1966, heading a Chartex train comprising SR Bulleid rolling stock. The train was the 3pm special to Waterloo, running via the branch to Tipton St Johns (and reversing at Sidmouth Junction). Note that the signals at this location are SR upper quadrants. *R. F. Roberts / Stephenson Locomotive Society*

Below: Running beside the delightful estuary of the River Exe between Starcross and Dawlish Warren on 4 August 1962 is clean, green 'Hymek' No D7005 with down inter-regional working 1V89. In common with the 'Warships' and 'Westerns' the 'Hymeks' had a maximum speed of 90mph, but they were regularly timed in excess of their nominal maximum. *John K. Morton*

From 1962 the 'Hymeks', in common with many other types, were sporting small yellow warning panels. On 3 August 1965 No D7027 passes the finial of the Dawlish advanced starting signal on its way west with a train for Kingswear. The 'Hymeks' cost £81,000 to build and turned the scales at 75½ tons. Each had a single 16-cylinder Maybach engine providing an output of 1,740hp, although the commonly quoted figure was 1,700hp. *Ian Allan Library*

The author has seen many thousands of photographs of trains in Cornwall over the past 40 years, but this is the only picture of a 'Hymek' at Penzance that has landed on his desk!
The class regularly worked into Cornwall (by way of example, colleague Maurice Dart's diary catalogues weekly appearances at St Austell in October 1964), but it seems that the railway-photographer fraternity were simply not on hand to capture such events. Pictured heading the 'Royal Duchy' to Paddington is No D7095, with soiled white window surrounds.
The photographer records the picture as having been taken on 3 October but does not show the year; probably this was 1964, given that this locomotive was noted at St Austell on that date. *Alan D. Francis*

Class 25s on Clay

Above: Built for light passenger- and freight-train duties the 73-ton, 1,250hp Sulzer-engined Class 25 Bo-Bos could be seen at work in many parts of the UK and together with the earlier Class 24s numbered nearly 500 locomotives, it being envisaged that they would be used in multiple on heavier trains. Class 25s arrived in the West Country in July 1971 to replace the Class 22 diesel-hydraulics, and their stay in Devon and Cornwall lasted until 1980, when they were ousted by the more powerful (and more reliable) Class 37s. Here, on 13 September 1979, No 25 206 tackles the steep climb up from Coombe Junction to Liskeard with loaded china-clay wagons from Moorswater. The train is passing beneath Liskeard Viaduct, which carries the main line from Plymouth to Penzance. *G. Roose*

Below: In pleasant late-afternoon lighting on 16 June 1978 a brace of Class 25s have just crossed the River Tamar, thereby passing from Cornwall into Devon, with ball-clay empties bound for the Heathfield branch. The early examples of the class originally had gangway connections fitted, hence the shallow centre window, but in later years these were sealed off and plated over. *Author*

Headboards

Above: When the 'Warship' classes of diesel-hydraulic began to take over the most prestigious named trains from their steam predecessors the same design of headboard was used; other leftovers from the age of steam included external train-indicator numbers and headcode discs. Now looking rather dated, the down 'Cornish Riviera Express' sweeps into Gwinear Road behind No D800 *Sir Brian Robertson* on 22 May 1959. At this time passengers could still change here for a branch line service to Helston. *Michael Mensing*

Below: One of the first three 2,000hp B-B 'Warships', No D801 *Vanguard,* pulls into Plymouth North Road station with the down 'Cornish Riviera Express' on 9 May 1959. This was during the period of transition from steam to diesel traction, and the station pilot that day was '64xx' 0-6-0PT No 6421, just visible on the left. The 'Warships' were delivered in green livery but from 1965 would be outshopped from overhaul in maroon. *Michael Mensing*

An immaculate ex-works No D805 *Benbow*, sporting the 'Cornish Riviera Express' headboard but without train-reporting numbers, climbs into Liskeard station on 23 May 1959. In their first few months of operation the 'Warships' suffered from severe bogie vibration at speeds above 80mph, which later resulted in the imposition of an 80mph speed limit, pending modifications.
Michael Mensing

Another of the named trains running on the WR in the late 1950s was the 'Torbay Express' from London Paddington to Torquay and Paignton (and return). The 'Warships' had a steam train-heating capability provided by either Spanner or Stone-Vapor boilers, while (perhaps surprisingly for a diesel-hydraulic design) every locomotive contained 2½ miles of electrical wiring! In this view what is believed to be No D804 *Cambrian* nears Shaldon with the up working in 1959.
Ian Allan Library

One of the original North British A1A-A1A 'Warships', No D602 *Bulldog,* at Penzance MPD in the early days of dieselisation. In view of the 'Royal Duchy' headboard there can be little doubt regarding the diagram to which the locomotive was rostered! Following delivery of the more successful B-B 'Warships' these heavy locomotives were usually to be found between Penzance and Plymouth. Each had cost £87,500 to build at 1957 values, but the five locomotives would see less than a decade of service. *M. G. Martin*

The various 'Warship' types did not have a complete monopoly of headboards, and on 19 August 1960 the up and down workings of the 'Cornishman' between Penzance and Plymouth were entrusted to NBL Type 2s Nos D6322 and D6312. Seen here is the down working, pausing at Bodmin Road station in an era when the branch line to Bodmin General was still open. *Roger A. Knott*

One of the great advantages of the new diesel era was the ability of a single 'Warship' to haul up to 10 coaches unaided over the South Devon banks between Newton Abbot and Plymouth; in the age of steam double-heading would have been mandatory with such a load. No D817 *Foxhound* was certainly unassisted as it arrived at Plymouth North Road with the down 'Cornish Riviera Express'. *A. A. Sellman*

Hydraulics to Kingswear

The first of four photographs showing the four main types of diesel-hydraulic locomotive that worked the line from Newton Abbot to Kingswear in the early days of dieselisation. A few down expresses from London to the West Country divided into Plymouth/Penzance and Torquay/Kingswear portions. On 4 May 1963 the four-coach portion of the 10.30am from Paddington nears Kingswear behind NBL Type 2 No D6306. *R. F. Roberts / Stephenson Locomotive Society*

Swindon-built 'Warship' No D830 *Majestic* was the only example to be fitted with a pair of Paxman engines, together rated at 2,270hp. The unique locomotive has just passed Goodrington Sands on its way to Kingswear (near to the mouth of the River Dart) on 30 August 1964. The 'Warships' regularly worked rosters that resulted in a *daily* mileage of over 400 miles, helped by an 800gal fuel tank and a fuel consumption of 1mpg! *G. F. Gillham*

Above: Heading six maroon coaches and a van forming the 17.30 Kingswear–Newton Abbot on 4 August 1964, 'Hymek' No D7089 gathers speed along the banks of the River Dart. Some 45 such locomotives were ordered initially, and BR took something of a chance in ordering a further 50 in July 1960 and a final six in the winter of 1961/2 before the design had been tried and tested. *R. E. Toop*

Below: More than a quarter of a century has now passed since the handsome Class 52s were withdrawn from BR service, but one of the 'celebrity' machines to have survived is No D1015 *Western Champion*. Uniquely, this locomotive once wore a livery of golden ochre, but on 6 August 1975 it was in grimy Rail blue as it worked empty stock from Goodrington sidings to form the 17.55 Paignton–Bristol. A family wait at the crossing gates — another delightful piece of railway infrastructure that has all but disappeared. *Brian Morrison*

Type 2s in Multiple

This double-page spread is a tribute to the work of Peter Treloar. The small 1,000/1,100hp NBL Type 2s were at home on short branch trains or local goods comprising a few wagons, but to cope with Class 1 passenger trains over the steep main-line gradients in both Devon and Cornwall they had to operate in multiple, with two (or very occasionally three) locomotives coupled together. This duo is passing Marazion station (near Penzance) with an up express in April 1960. The attractive station was to close six months later. *P. Q. Treloar*

Pulling into the junction station of Gwinear Road are two early 1,000hp examples of the class, Nos D6304 and D6303, working the 10.5am Penzance–Manchester on 19 September 1959. The pair were then only three months old. Over their first three years of service No D6304 would average 40,000 miles per annum and No D6303 33,000 miles — quite reasonable for small Type 2 locomotives. *P. Q. Treloar*

This splendid panorama shows the coastline and sea defences at Penzance, while on the far left can be seen the overall roof of the station. With headcode discs glowing, 1,000hp pioneers Nos D6302 and D6301 are seen leaving with a maroon rake of MR coaches and vans forming the 10.5am to Manchester on 23 September 1959. *P. Q. Treloar*

Back in September 1959 the NBL Type 2s were something of a novelty, but some of these small B-Bs were to be residents in the Royal Duchy for a further 12 years. Here Nos D6302 and D6301 head a down train of very mixed coaching stock at Gwinear Road on 19 September 1959. Gwinear Road was the junction for the Helston branch, until closure of the latter to passenger traffic in November 1962. The branch struggled on as a freight-only line before complete abandonment in October 1964, when Gwinear Road also closed. *P. Q. Treloar*

Full marks to the photographer for persevering during a heavy April shower in 1960! Passing Marazion in pouring rain are Nos D6309 and D6315 with a down six-coach passenger train. Note the old box vans in the goods yard, itself long since abandoned. The original batch of NBL Type 2s cost £55,000 each to build at 1959 values and the later machines £61,700. The locomotives had a fuel consumption of 1.45 miles per gallon. *P. Q. Treloar*

It has always been very difficult to photograph five locomotives in action simultaneously at Truro, but on 21 September 1959 Peter Treloar achieved such a feat. The down main-line signal is 'off' for Nos D6301 and D6302 with the 7.45am Newton Abbot–Penzance, while on the left Prairie tank No 5536 arrives with the 10.35am branch train from Falmouth. (One wonders if anybody was sitting in the solitary non-smoking First-class compartment!) In the background another early diesel arrival shunts the yard while 'County' 4-6-0 No 1007 *County of Brecknock* waits for the road with a down fitted freight. *P. Q. Treloar*

Class 45s on the Sea Wall

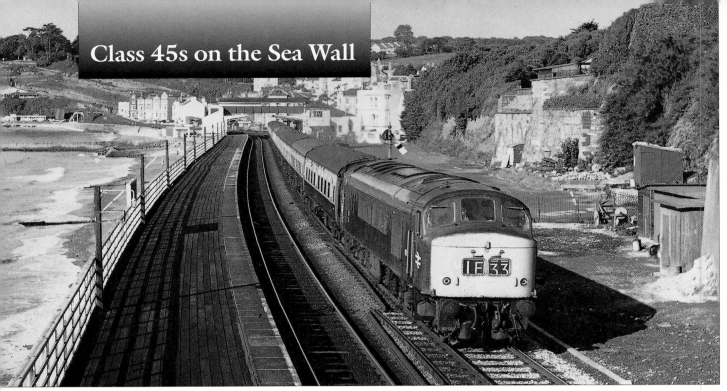

Above: The 2,500hp BR/Sulzer Type 4 (Class 45) 'Peak' diesel-electrics were introduced towards the end of 1960, and by November 1961 a number of these 16-wheeled 1Co-Co1 locomotives had been transferred to the former MR Bristol Barrow Road depot, where they replaced some of the three-cylinder 4-6-0 'Jubilee' steam locomotives, working primarily between Bristol, Birmingham and beyond. Although the class occasionally ventured southwest from Bristol an item in a 1969 magazine observed that No D28 had been *unusually* noted at Plymouth. A few months after that observation, and sporting the 1E33 headcode, No 121 leaves Dawlish at the head of the 07.20 Paignton–Leeds on 23 June 1970. *Leslie Riley*

Below: The view of Dawlish from the station overbridge in September 1985, with a Class 45/1 heading a down eight-coach passenger train along the sea wall. The '45/1' sub-class was created in 1973 by converting steam-heating locomotives (thereafter known as '45/0s') to electric train heating, in order to heat the latest generation of passenger coaches. The signalbox is now disused, and there have recently been disputes concerning preservation of this listed structure, which would now seem to be safe from demolition. *Author*

Above: Although the location is not strictly on the famous 'sea wall', no book on Devon's railways would be complete without at least one photograph of the small harbour at Cockwood, between Dawlish Warren and Starcross, on the estuary of the River Exe. Heading the 15.10 Plymouth–Manchester on 4 August 1976 is No 45 012 (originally No D108). In their early days in the South West the 'Peaks' tended to work long-distance inter-regional trains to/from the Eastern Region, including the famous 'Cornishman'; destinations included Leeds, Bradford, York and Newcastle. *Les Bertram*

Below: The absence of an ETH jumper cable shows that this 'Peak' is a steam-heating Class 45/0. Running along the famous sea wall in glorious conditions is No 45 043 (originally D58) *The King's Own Border Regiment* heading a Derby–Plymouth train in July 1975. These substantial locomotives turned the scales at a massive 136 tons, but with weight spread across eight axles their route availability was not compromised. The class were banned west of Bristol from October 1985, but for many years they were solid workhorses in Devon and Cornwall. *I. J. Hodson*

The cattle grazing in the fields of Devon and Cornwall produce the essential ingredient for a large variety of dairy products, and in terms of rail transport the most important was milk itself. For many decades this was conveyed by rail to the capital in 3,000gal six-wheeled tank wagons. There were a large number of important sidings at St Erth, Dalcoath, Lostwithiel, Saltash, Totnes, Torrington and Hemyock, to name but a few. This Class 47's 2,580hp is hardly required for just two milk tankers, seen arriving at Lostwithiel in May 1976. *Author*

The author spent the entire night of 8/9 July 1975 on the platforms of Plymouth North Road station and witnessed many interesting freight workings, including this Class 6 milk train, seen just after arrival from Cornwall. Waiting to tackle the South Devon banks is Class 52 'Western' No D1034 *Western Dragoon.* Sadly the locomotive would be withdrawn from service just 12 weeks later. *Author*

In the days when Tiverton Junction station was still open, albeit no longer a junction for passenger trains, Class 22 No D6333 in BR blue livery arrives with milk empties for the United Dairies creamery at Hemyock. The line to Tiverton closed in October 1964, but the Culm Valley line to Hemyock, closed to passengers from September 1963, survived for some years as a freight-only branch before the M5 motorway bisected the trackbed. Photographed on 12 September 1970, the junction station would eventually close in May 1986 upon the opening of the new Tiverton Parkway facility. *Author*

The Cornish milk traffic went to Acton Yard, Kensington and West Ealing, and during 1956 no less than 19 million gallons of milk left Cornwall for London! Each tanker would gross to 28 tons when loaded. On 15 June 1978 the milk output for conveyance by rail from the St Erth and Lostwithiel creameries amounted to 39,000 gallons, transported in these wonderful (and long since extinct) vacuum-braked six-wheeled tank wagons. Entering Devon and passing the redundant signalbox that formerly controlled traffic over the Royal Albert Bridge across the River Tamar is No 50 044 *Exeter*. All milk traffic now travels by road. *Author*

Brush Type 4s on Freight

Pure nostalgia. Class 47 No 47 110 has long disappeared from locomotive lists, wagonloads of domestic coal have ceased, brake vans no longer appear on freight trains and St Austell goods yard, which opened in 1931, has been closed for many years.

On 4 June 1981 the goods has just arrived from St Blazey and is about to reverse from the down main line to the up so that the wagons can be propelled into the goods yard. *Author*

The Class 47s have been versatile performers in Devon and Cornwall since 1967 — at the time of writing a 37-year reign. They have appeared on every type of train, ranging from main-line expresses and overnight sleepers to postal and parcel trains and humble freights of every description. One of the more interesting workings, sadly now defunct, was the Mondays-only United Kingdom Fertilizer (UKF) train from Truro to Ince & Elton. On 21 November 1983 No 47 101 powers up the gradient into Bodmin Road with five wagons in tow. *Author*

One of the most glorious and memorable vistas on the Cornish main line can be enjoyed on the marvellous journey up the Glynn Valley from Bodmin Road to Doublebois. Passing through the avenue of deciduous trees on the approach to Penadlake Viaduct on a wonderful April morning is the mixed 09.35 St Blazey–Severn Tunnel Junction freight, hauled by No 47 125. The train will shortly be climbing a gradient of 1 in 58. *Author*

A long study of an Ordnance Survey map and a very long walk takes the more intrepid photographer to this excellent vantage-point on a small peninsula east of the 1907/8-built St Germans Viaduct, visible in the background. Heading towards Plymouth with the 09.32 St Blazey–Severn Tunnel Junction is all-blue 'Duff' No 47 249. The train is on a deviation line that was ready for service in 1908. *Author*

Devon Branches

Over the years numerous branch lines in both Devon and Cornwall have closed. One of the more interesting locations was Halwill Junction, which although in a rural setting was served by trains on three different routes. The direct line through the station ran from Okehampton to Bude, the North Cornwall Railway branched off to Wadebridge and Padstow, and the North Devon & Cornwall Junction line headed north to Torrington. The line to Torrington closed in 1965, and those to Bude and Wadebridge were shut the following year. The single-car DMU in the down bay platform will make for Wadebridge, while the Bude connection is on the right. *David Lawrence/ M. Dart collection*

The 7½-mile branch from Tiverton Junction to Hemyock had two intermediate stations, at Uffculme and Culmstock. Known as the Culm Valley branch, the line opened in May 1876 and closed to passengers on 9 September 1963; as mentioned previously, it soldiered on until the early 1970s for milk traffic, although a mill was also served for some time. In late-afternoon sunshine Class 22 No D6333 returns from Hemyock and prepares to cross the minor road at Uffculme on 12 September 1970. *Author*

Along the LSWR main line from Salisbury to Exeter were a number of branches serving seaside resorts, including Lyme Regis, Seaton, Sidmouth and Exmouth, but all save the last have now closed. Passengers for Seaton would change at Seaton Junction, where this scene was recorded in the early 1960s. In early green livery with cream 'whiskers', the DMU at the curving junction platform will shortly leave for Seaton. Note the goods wagons in the background. The Seaton branch closed in March 1966.
M. Dart collection

Passengers for Kingsbridge once changed trains at Brent on the GWR/WR main line, but that is now a matter of history. The charming branch had camping coaches at several intermediate stations, such as Gara Bridge and Loddiswell, seen here. The small boy is probably on holiday in this August 1961 view of single car No W55013 leaving for the terminus. The branch was to close just two years later, in September 1963.
M. Dart collection

The delightful LSWR terminus at Sidmouth comprised a single platform with two faces, in addition to the usual infrastructure, including a large goods shed (seen here on the left). Trains worked to/from Sidmouth Junction on the main line, but at Tipton St John's the branch joined the route from Exmouth and Budleigh Salterton. In the early days of 'dieselisation' a two-car unit waits to leave the seaside terminus. The Sidmouth branch would close with effect from 6 March 1967.
M. Dart collection

St Erth Scenes

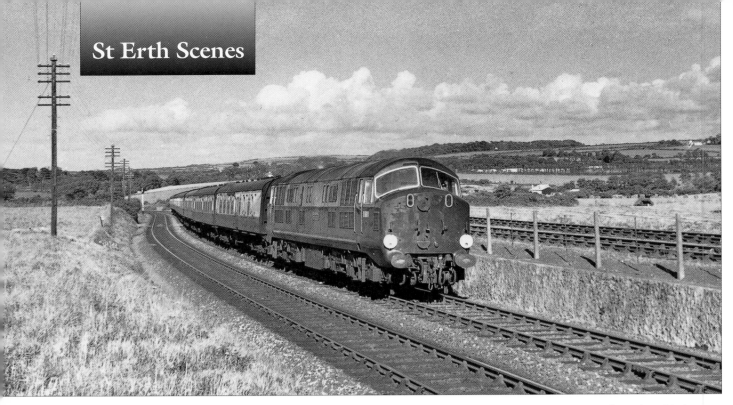

Above: Even today St Erth remains the junction station for St Ives, the St Ives branch being one of the few survivors of the Beeching era. At the beginning of the 21st century the station area still retains most of its manual semaphore signalling. On an idyllic summer's day back in 1958 A1A-A1A 'Warship' No D601 *Ark Royal* climbs the last few yards into St Erth station with a down express. The stop at St Erth will prompt a flurry of activity as many of the passengers change for Lelant, Carbis Bay and St Ives. *P. Q. Treloar*

Below: There is little doubt that in retrospect the B-B 'Warships' were not appreciated when they were plentiful on the Cornish main line. One of the crack expresses from the North East of England was train 1V70 — the 'Cornishman' — seen here rolling into the delightful St Erth station on 20 June 1970 behind a very clean NBL/MAN-engined Class 43, No 854 *Tiger*. Built in 1961, this locomotive would be withdrawn in 1971 and scrapped in 1972, having covered some 688,000 miles in service. *Author*

Above: St Erth had a very busy goods yard on the up side and more sidings on the down side just before the station. There was also a refuge siding, used during shunting operations and to berth goods trains destined for the wharves at Hayle. In this charming view, recorded on 14 September 1980, the guard is signalling to the driver of Class 25 No 25 223, which will propel the entire formation along the main line for nearly two miles. The load comprises two box vans and six fuel tankers — plus, of course, the mandatory brake van. *Author*

Below: For several years during the early 1980s local trains between Plymouth and Penzance (and a few workings from Exeter) were locomotive-hauled. Such workings were generally shared between Class 47s and 50s, although occasionally a 'Peak' would be used, and with at least 2,500hp available the station-to-station timings could be quite impressive! Arriving at St Erth from Plymouth with five Mk 1 coaches on 9 November 1985 is No 47 486. Note the down sidings on the right. *Author*

Class 52 Headcodes

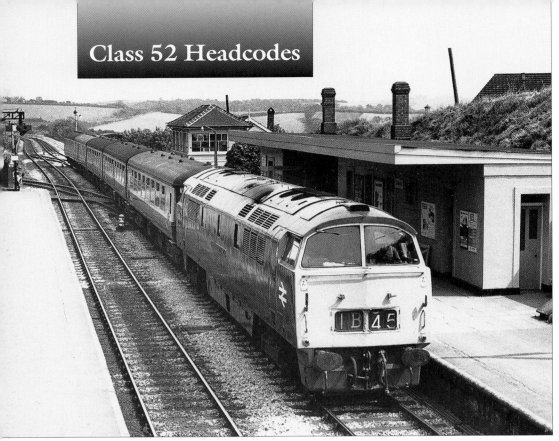

During 1975 the headcode 1B45 denoted the down 'Cornish Riviera Express'. Passing the now demolished down side station building at Liskeard on 4 July 1975 is 'Western' Class 52 No D1053 *Western Patriarch*. Half of the train from Paddington, including the catering facilities, has been left at Plymouth, just five coaches continuing through to Penzance. *Author*

From the beginning of 1976 headcode panels were effectively abolished, but until the headcode boxes were blanked off many locomotives had the blinds turned to '0000'. In the case of the 'Westerns' many blinds were turned to show the actual locomotive number, as here with No D1070 *Western Gauntlet*, which has travelled well over 200 miles from Paddington as it rolls down into Lostwithiel in May 1976. *Author*

Above: Use of the letter 'Z' in train-identification codes always signified a special train, mostly Chartex and Adex (respectively chartered and advertised excursions) workings. On 15 July 1969 headcode 1Z15 was applied to a six-coach troop train from Gloucester to Plymouth. Headed by No D1011 *Western Thunderer*, the special passes Totnes on the down through road. In later years locomotives would be given all-yellow ends to aid visibility, but adoption of the tried and tested North American practice of using powerful headlights would take much longer. *G. F. Gillham*

Below: Respryn Bridge, beside the River Fowey, has always been a favourite photographic vantage-point for up morning trains, but sadly sights such as this can no longer be experienced. With an unbelievably tidy and weed-free lineside, train 1A19 from Penzance to Paddington, headed by Class 52 No D1011 *Western Thunderer,* gallops towards Bodmin Road, where the train will stop to pick up, on 4 July 1975. As a general rule on the Paddington–Penzance route headcodes with the letter 'A' denoted an up train, while the inclusion of a 'B' or 'C' described down workings. *Author*

The Sulzer-engined Brush Type 4s (later known as Class 47s) appeared on the WR from 1963, when Nos D1682/3 arrived at Old Oak Common in London. Predictably it was not long before the class appeared in the West Country, although it was only upon the mass withdrawal of the 'Warships' that the class arrived in really large numbers. The locomotives were painted in an attractive two-tone green livery, shown here by No D1920 (later 47 243), approaching Dainton Tunnel on 20 July 1973 with a down freight. *G. F. Gillham*

Shunters aside, in terms of longevity of service in Devon and Cornwall the Class 47s and their variants now hold the record, having seen off all other classes of diesel locomotive. With over 40 years of service on BR and 37 in the West Country they even rival most classes of steam locomotive, except the Beattie well tanks that worked the Wenford Goods line in Cornwall from 1893 until 1963! Passing two fine semaphore signal gantries on the approach to Newton Abbot on 10 June 1969 is No D1542 (later ETH-fitted No 47 430) with the 17.00 Paignton–Paddington. *L. Riley*

Weedkillers

In the past all lines in Devon and Cornwall normally received an annual visit from the weedkilling train. Considerably more effort was put into lineside maintenance than is presently the case, although to be fair in the days of steam regular small fires caused by the emission of hot cinders helped control embankment foliage. On 16 May 1971 the (by then) freight-only line from Bodmin Road to Bodmin General received a visit from the weedkiller powered by Class 22 No D6326. On the left is a Hawksworth coach of the Great Western Society (which at the time occupied a siding to undertake restoration work), while on the right is a 'Presflo' wagon, used for slate-dust traffic from Delabole Quarry. *M. Dart collection*

In bright sunshine following a heavy shower Class 25 No 25 225 pulls into the up platform at Liskeard on 15 May 1976 with the annual weedkilling run, the '0000' headcode giving a clue to the year. The two companies most associated with weedkilling trains in this era were Chipmans and Fisons. The original Liskeard station, at street level (top right), has recently been refurbished. *Author*

'Tis Rainin'

Above: It is slightly amusing to the regular visitor to Devon and Cornwall to look at the holiday posters and guide books showing nothing but golden sunny scenes. The reality is that, whatever the time of year, moisture-laden clouds rolling off the Atlantic Ocean regularly deposit their contents over the two counties! The floods at Lynmouth in August 1952 and Boscastle in August 2004 are testimony to such events. On 9 November 1985 the down newspaper train was running very late, but it is not known whether the atrocious conditions were a factor. In appalling weather No 47 575 *City of Hereford* pauses at Redruth while the BRUTE trolleys are loaded with papers. *Author*

Below: Another wet day in Cornwall, and the only place for the author to shelter while still managing to photograph trains was under the awnings of Truro station. With the flagstones reflecting the conditions one of the last 'Westerns' to survive, No D1041 *Western Prince*, arrives with the 9.30 Paddington–Penzance express on 17 May 1976. The lines (on the left) to the erstwhile goods yard have since been lifted, while the industrial siding (right) has also disappeared. *Author*

The author could never be accused of being a fair-weather photographer, even if he was 'hiding' under the awnings of Par station on 2 October 1985! In the wettest conditions ever experienced in Cornwall, with a deluge that lasted many hours, the headlight of Class 50 No 50 020 *Revenge* pierces the gloom with the 09.36 Liverpool–Penzance inter-regional working. The 105mm f1.8 Nikkor lens was at maximum aperture, and only 1/250sec shutter speed was possible on 400ASA Ilford XP1 film. *Author*

Although headcode boxes did not feature in the original designs for the class, BR insisted in the 1960s that the new Class 50 fleet should have these mounted at roof level, which alteration is considered by some to have spoiled the looks of the type. This and the following photographs show the headcode panels in a number of different modes. In what could be an extension of wet-weather scenes an English Electric Class 50 whines its way into St Austell station with a down train on 18 May 1976; the headcode panel shows '0000', the requirement to display train-identity headcodes having ceased with effect from 31 December 1975. *Author*

There was a brief period in the history of the Class 50s when the locomotives had been named and had their headcode panels masked to display two white marker lights but had not yet been refurbished. During this time, on 2 April 1979, No 50 047 *Swiftsure* arrives at Liskeard spot on time with the 12.24 Penzance–Paddington. Note the clay hood wagons in the (now lifted) sidings. *Author*

The Class 50s did not arrive in the West in any number until 1975, so the use of headcodes in Devon and Cornwall lasted only a matter of months, making such photographs quite scarce. Disturbing the few residents who live in the immediate environs of Menheniot station (which is over a mile from the village of that name) in 1975 is this booming Class 50 with the 1V76 Liverpool–Penzance. The attractive stone station was latterly unmanned and ultimately burned down. *Author*

Upon refurbishment, effected between 1979 and 1983 and entailing numerous mechanical and electrical modifications, the Class 50s were fitted with powerful quartz-halogen headlights, which supplemented the existing roof-level marker lights; the erstwhile headcode panel was now overplated. Most locomotives emerged in 'large logo' livery, generally with light-grey roofs, although a few had dark-blue roofs. Sporting the former, No 50 029 *Renown* is seen through a 200mm lens pounding across Tresulgan Viaduct, east of Menheniot, with the 10.45 Penzance–Paddington on 11 August 1983. The days of spending nearly six hours in a Mk 1 coach have now gone forever. *Author*

Swindon-built

The Swindon-built 'Cross-Country' diesel multiple-units were delivered for service between 1957 and 1960. Some 130 power cars were constructed, each with a pair of 150hp engines, giving a total of 600hp for a typical working unit. Later designated Class 120, these units worked throughout the British mainland, including the West Country. With its erstwhile headcode panel plated over, unit No P552, coupled to a single car of Class 121 or 122, approaches St Erth with a branch train from St Ives on 16 June 1978. *Author*

This three-car Class 120 DMU was encountered on the Falmouth branch on 20 June 1970. In those leisurely days the author was allowed to leave the train, grab a photograph from the board crossing at Penryn station and rejoin! In addition to train 2C53, points of note (which date the picture) are the passing loop, the gas lamp on the platform and the GWR station seat, all now consigned to history. *Author*

Candy Stripe

Above: Over the years there have been numerous changes and experiments to rolling-stock livery, although none compares with the rich variety of colour schemes currently being applied by independent railway-operating and leasing companies. In 1979 it was decided to paint refurbished DMUs white with a central blue stripe — totally impractical for keeping exterior paintwork looking clean. On 4 July 1979 a Derby Class 116 unit, with car No W50868 leading, leaves Totnes as the 16.10 Barnstaple–Plymouth. *Brian Morrison*

Below: The new DMU colour scheme became known as 'candy stripe' livery, and by 9 June 1980 Metropolitan-Cammell Class 101 unit No B804 had been so treated. Having worked down as the 16.50 Plymouth–Par stopper, the three-car set returned empty as the 18.40 Par–Plymouth ECS, seen passing a down train at Bodmin Road station (later renamed Bodmin Parkway). *Author*

Warships at St Davids

Above: The 'Warships' were not confined to main-line trains in the West, being regular performers on the line to Barnstaple and (before it closed in 1970) Ilfracombe. Posing on 23 August 1968 beneath a truly splendid gantry of lower-quadrant semaphore signals with finials on wooden posts is No D814 *Dragon*. The train is the 13.25 Exeter St Davids–Ilfracombe. *David Birch*

Below: One of the all-time favourite places for observing trains in the county of Devon is Exeter St Davids. Trains arrive and depart in four directions — north to Taunton (and beyond to Paddington or Bristol), east to Salisbury (and beyond to Waterloo or Southampton), south to Newton Abbot (and beyond to Paignton or Plymouth/Penzance) and northwest to Crediton (and thence to Barnstaple or Okehampton). With its BR logo amidships rather than on the cab ends No 826 *Jupiter* departs with the 09.30 Paddington–Paignton on 2 August 1971. *David Wharton*

Above: Following the end of steam on the Waterloo–Salisbury–Exeter route in 1965/6 B-B 'Warships' took over most services, taking the class onto SR metals on a daily basis. Reliability was sometimes an issue, but the position was exacerbated by the singling of parts of the route between Pinhoe and Wilton, which increased delays whenever a failure occurred. No 811 *Daring* departs from Platform 2 with the 16.00 for Waterloo on 1 September 1971. *John Cooper-Smith*

Below: SR Class 33s, which already worked regularly over the LSWR main line, particularly on the SO Brighton–Exeter St Davids 'out and back' turn (which often produced double-headed 'Cromptons'), replaced 'Warships' over the route from 4 October 1971. This was a disastrous month for the 'Warships', no fewer that 25 of the class being withdrawn, in addition to those condemned earlier. Here, on 2 August 1971, No 832 *Onslaught* waits to depart with the 14.33 to Waterloo. Happily this particular locomotive would subsequently be preserved. *David Wharton*

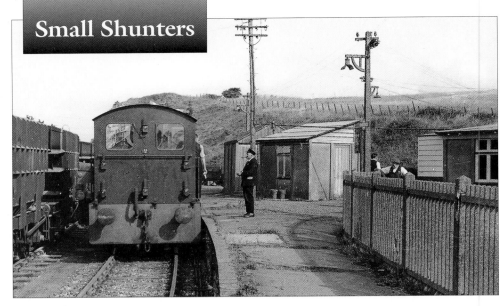

Small Shunters

Although diesel traction is featured here there is almost a steam-age 'feel' about this scene, no doubt enhanced by the green shunting locomotive without warning stripes and the pipe-smoking railwayman on the SR platform at Plymstock. The 204hp Drewry 0-6-0 (later Class 04) is one of the '112xx' series, Nos 11225/7-9 all being allocated to 83H (the SR Plymouth Friary depot) in the early 1960s. The line in the foreground once continued to Turnchapel, this branch having closed to passengers from September 1951. *M. Dart collection*

A most interesting branch in the Plymouth area is that from Plymouth Friary to Cattewater, which remains open today, the traffic flow comprising mainly petroleum- and bitumen-based products. Of particular interest was the Esso terminal (since closed), reached by means of a small tunnel at the end of the branch. With a wooden wagon being used as a match wagon between the shunter and the fuel tankers for visibility purposes, Class 03 No D2134 leaves the Esso yard on 25 October 1971. *M. Dart*

Plymouth Friary was the main LSWR/SR terminus in the Plymouth area, but once the WR took over the control of most of the SR lines in the South West it became superfluous, being a duplication of the WR's North Road station; it finally closed to passengers in September 1958. BR Swindon 0-6-0 (later Class 03) No D2178 was photographed at Friary during a visit by the Plymouth Railway Circle in 1966. *M. Dart collection*

Above: During the early/mid-1960s the small 204hp 0-6-0 shunters (later Classes 03 and 04) were part of the motive-power scene in both Devon and Cornwall, but within a few years of their introduction the majority of station goods yards and general marshalling yards closed, as wagonload freight dried up, such that many of these locomotives had very short lives. No D2129 is seen beside the coaling ramp at St Blazey MPD. *Author's collection*

Below: This terrific shot shows BR Swindon 0-6-0 shunter No D2131 coupled to a very curious collection of rail vehicles at Exeter St Davids station, probably *c*1960. On the wall of the station is a poster depicting one of the original A1A-A1A 'Warships', which began working express trains in the area from June 1958. By the mid-1960s small diesel-mechanical shunters would be extinct in the South West, although the more powerful diesel-electric shunters (later Class 08) continued to find employment. *M. Dart collection*

NBLs on Cornish Branches

Above: Few corners of the rail network in Devon and Cornwall are beyond the reach of the intrepid railway photographer. On the remote line from Nanpean Wharf to Drinnick Mill Class 22 No D6315 brings up a long load of china-clay wagons, which contain both powdered and bagged clay, on 16 May 1969. Note the white wheel rims, caused by clay slurry on sharply curved sidings at minor clay works; also the giant clay tips in the background. *Stephenson Locomotive Society*

Below: A quite delightful scene featuring No D6315 employed on duties entirely different from those depicted in the previous photograph. Leaving Perranporth on 4 June 1961 on the now defunct line from Chacewater is the 4.35pm to Newquay, consisting of a single coach with two First- and four Third-class compartments. The line would close to passengers from 4 February 1963. *J. C. Beckett*

Another rarity is this view of a goods train on the Falmouth branch. Shunting the yard at Penryn on 2 September 1970 is No D6322. Note the box vans in the yard (left) and on the main branch (right). The locomotive would remain in service for a further 12 months, being withdrawn in October 1971 and broken up at Swindon in May 1972. Although the Falmouth branch is still open today, goods trains are a thing of the past, despite attempts to find a regular source of freight traffic.
Michael H. C. Baker

With 450gal fuel tanks, a 500gal boiler-water capacity and a top speed of 75mph, the little NBL Type 2s rarely worked up Class 1 passenger trains beyond Exeter, line speeds in Devon and Cornwall generally ensuring that their lack of pace was no restriction. No D6342 is seen at Newquay on 15 June 1964. Note the BR 'lion and wheel' crest just below the roofline. *Les Elsey*

Above: As part of the National Traction Plan a new policy was announced whereby BR intended to standardise on diesel-electric classes, to the detriment of diesel-hydraulics. This hastened the replacement of diesel-hydraulic classes in the South West: main-works overhauls on the Class 43 NBL 'Warships' ceased almost immediately, and during 1971/2 1,250hp Sulzer-engined Class 25s replaced the 1,100hp NBL/MAN Class 22s. Seen between semaphore signals and Dawlish Warren signalbox is No 25 048 with an Exeter–Paignton train in 1978. *Author*

Below: Although regarded initially as freight locomotives the Class 25s soon proved very useful on Class 2 passenger trains, the Summer 1976 timetable including many local services between Exeter and Paignton or Plymouth that were diagrammed for 'Rat' haulage rather than DMU formations. No 25 220 leaves Dawlish with the 19.30 Exeter St Davids–Paignton on 23 June. *G. F. Gillham*

Above: From the start of 'dieselisation' the line from Exeter to Barnstaple had been worked largely by DMUs. However, certain trains were locomotive-hauled, perhaps the most notable being a Saturdays-only through train from Paddington to the North Devon market town. In May 1980 it was the turn of No 25 057 to haul the train, the Class 25 having taken over from a larger and more powerful locomotive at Exeter. Although the line is not steeply graded the load of 10 Mk 1 coaches would make the little Bo-Bo work hard over its 39-mile journey. *Author*

Below: The SO through train from Paddington to Barnstaple had to change direction at Exeter St Davids, where a Type 2 locomotive would take over from Type 4 power, thereby avoiding the need for the original train engine to run round. On 26 July 1980 No 25 048 produces a plume of exhaust as it departs with the 09.48 Paddington–Barnstaple holiday train. Between 1979 and 1981 the Class 25s were replaced in the West Country by Class 37s. *Les Bertram*

The Looe Branch

Top left: The Looe branch has a long and interesting history, fully described in the author's OPC volume *Branches and Byways: Cornwall.* From 1846 minerals were brought down from the hills around Caradon and Cheesewring to Moorswater, where they were transferred to the 1828-built canal to Looe for onward shipment; the branch from Moorswater down to Looe opened in September 1879. Approaching St Keyne station with the 17.10 Looe–Liskeard on 10 June 1981 — yet another wet summer's day — is three-car Class 118 suburban unit No P463. *Author*

Lower left: The original branch line between Moorswater and Looe did not connect with the main Plymouth–Penzance line until 1901, when a steeply graded (1-in-40) loop line from Liskeard to Coombe Junction was opened. The configuration meant that all trains between Liskeard and Looe had to reverse at Coombe Junction. Having just descended from Liskeard, the driver of the 08.04 from Liskeard exchanges single-line tokens with the Coombe Junction signalman on 16 April 1981. Within a few days the signalbox would close, leaving the guard to change the points for the reversal under the auspices of the Liskeard main-line signalman. *Author*

Right: The ride down to Looe is very picturesque as the railway follows the river and the remains of the old Liskeard & Looe Union Canal from Coombe Junction to the branch terminus. Looe can be very congested in summer, and a 'park and ride' scheme operates on the branch line. A recently transferred 'bubble car', No W55033, still sporting a Welsh Dragon transfer on the front end, heads south from Coombe Junction with the 09.12 Liskeard–Looe on 1 October 1985. *Author*

Around Okehampton

In the 1960s and 1970s the former LSWR/SR routes in Devon suffered very badly in terms of line closures. It would be easy to blame these on the one-time rival WR, which had assumed control of the lines, but there is little doubt that many were unprofitable. Okehampton was an important LSWR/SR railway centre, the main line between Exeter and Plymouth passing through the town and other services running to Bude and Wadebridge. NBL Type 2s Nos D6302 and D6303 pass Crediton with the 2.45pm Plymouth–Exeter Central on 18 July 1959. *S. C. Nash*

Gradually the lines west of Okehampton closed, except for the line to Meldon Quarry. Okehampton became the end of the line for passengers but remained under threat of closure. The line struggled on until June 1972, when the Okehampton–Yeoford (Coleford Junction) section closed — just at the start of the summer season! Here, on 3 April 1969, passengers spill out of the limited accommodation provided by single car No W55029, which has just arrived as the 13.35 from Exeter. *G. F. Gillham*

Once all passenger trains had ceased the line through Okehampton remained open for ballast trains from Meldon Quarry, which in the 1980s was extremely busy supplying BR's own needs. On 20 October 1985, with the by-now closed station looking surprisingly intact, Class 33s Nos 33 002 and 33 107 pass through with a heavy train of 'Seacow' ballast wagons grossing in excess of 1,000 tons. *Author*

On 3 April 1969, before closure to passengers, there was still a goods service to Okehampton (note the wagons in the sidings), but this ragbag of old empty vacuum-braked ballast wagons was destined for Meldon Quarry. Passing a tall SR lattice upper-quadrant signal is Class 52 'Western' No D1067 *Western Druid*. Passenger services would be partially reinstated in the late 1990s, when subsidised trains started to run to/from Exeter on certain summer Sundays. *G. F. Gillham*

One Cornish freight working that continues to run to this day is the delivery of fuel tankers to Long Rock (near Penzance) for railway use, the train now running weekly to/from Tavistock Junction, Plymouth. The 1,250hp Class 25s were ideally suited to such work, No 25 207 being seen hauling eight empty tanks and a flat car past Respryn Bridge, near Bodmin Road station, on 14 June 1978. *Author*

Plenty of nostalgia for brake-van fans as coal empties from Long Rock make their way up the Cornish main line at Tomperrow towards Truro and St Blazey on 12 June 1980 behind No 25 225. The brake van was a home on wheels for the train guard during a shift; there were bench seats by the observation side windows, a stove to warm the van on cold days (hence the chimney) and keep the tea warm, a veranda at each end from which to observe proceedings and an individual door at each end controlling access to the cabin, while a metal slide bar provided security and prevented railway employees falling from the platform. *Author*

The proceedings at Lostwithiel on a normally sleepy Sunday morning were livened up on 11 June 1978, when a heavy train of rails passed through behind a brace of Class 25s. A Class 8 working, the train comprised numerous lifted track panels and necessitated the use of two brake tenders (marshalled immediately behind the locomotives) and a brake van. Nos 25 155 and 25 207 are seen heading for Tavistock Junction. The grand old Cornwall Railway station building would later be demolished — an act of official vandalism. *Author*

The Class 25s were truly 'Jacks of all trades', working every type of train in Devon and Cornwall, including, on busy summer Saturdays, Class 1 expresses, albeit normally double-headed. On 12 June 1978 No 25 052, one of the early locomotives with original bodyside design, was employed on relatively mundane duties as it worked a down engineers' train past Crugwallins, west of Burngullow. Again, a four-wheeled brake van brings up the rear, even though the train is probably vacuum-braked rather than unfitted. *Author*

Devon Gantries

Above: Although inevitably the primary focus of 'Diesel Days' is motive power the secondary subjects of interest must be rolling stock and the changing railway infrastructure, especially signalling. Over the years wonderful signalling centres have been abolished under modernisation schemes. The down end of Newton Abbot station was, until May 1987, one of many classic views in Devon, with a splendid gantry giving a clear indication of when a train was due to depart from or pass through the station. Class 50 No 50 043 *Eagle* is seen departing with the 13.18 Paddington–Paignton on 4 July 1984. *Author*

Top right: At the up end of the Newton Abbot complex was this delightful gantry of lower-quadrant semaphores, which were attached to wooden posts *vice* the normal tubular metal examples such as the advanced starter visible on the left. In some welcome afternoon sunshine No 50 007 *Sir Edward Elgar* arrives with a down express from Paddington in July 1984. *Author*

Lower left: Armed with a lineside photographic pass, which in the old days was readily available through formal channels, the author ventured over the bridge spanning the River Exe to obtain this shot of Class 45/1 'Peak' No 45 133 departing Exeter St Davids with the 09.22 Newcastle–Penzance on 20 April 1985. The WR gantry includes home, distant and shunt signals, although it is interesting to note that two of the three distant signals are 'fixed'. A broadly similar but wooden GWR gantry at this location was replaced in 1975. *Author*

Lower right: It is doubly satisfying when a splendid signal gantry can be photographed with unusual motive power passing by. Here, in September 1984, a pair of Class 37s (or 'Siphons'), No 37 219 leading, approach Exeter St Davids from the north, with perhaps half a dozen 'bashers' leaning from the windows of the leading carriages. The entire signalling system at Exeter St Davids was converted to MAS colour-light signalling during the early 1980s. *Author*

Top left: Glimpsed through the abandoned up-side goods yard at Whimple, Devon, on 18 November 1983 was Class 50 No 50 011 *Centurion* with a Waterloo–Exeter working. This locomotive would be the first of the fifty Class 50s to be withdrawn, on 24 February 1987. The sidings at Whimple were latterly used for loading the seasonal apple harvest from Whiteway's nearby orchards, the fruit being used in the cider-making process. New houses now cover the entire site. *Author*

Lower left: Trains are on the move 24 hours per day, but night shots appear only occasionally in books and magazines. Pausing at Axminster, the first/last station in Devon on the former LSWR main line, with the 16.18 Exeter St Davids–Waterloo on 21 November 1983 is No 50 050 *Fearless*. Between Pinhoe and Yeovil Junction (a distance of more than 46 miles) the line is now single-track, except for passing loops at Honiton and Chard. *Author*

Right: Although there is a popular expression that proclaims 'Glorious Devon' — which it is — there should also be a 'Delightful Cornwall', because in parts the scenery and the topography are equally attractive. This view, from a rural lane near Coombe Junction, was possible before a modern streetlamp was erected plumb in the middle of the scene! With an ancient farm in the foreground, Class 47 No 47 243 crosses the magnificent Moorswater Viaduct with a down train on 11 August 1983. *Author*

Mixed Double-headers

Above: In the days of locomotive haulage Devon and Cornwall were renowned for double-headed trains. In many cases double-heading arose from operational requirements rather than the need for additional horsepower. This and the following photographs show some interesting combinations. On 18 May 1976, when the down station building at Lostwithiel was being demolished, Class 47 No 47 267 and an unidentified Class 46 'Peak' were paired on an up express. Again, the headcode status acts as a clue to the year. *Author*

Below: Although in general terms most classes of motive power were capable of double-heading with sister locomotives, often different classes of motive power were not compatible. Classes 50 and 47 could not work together in multiple, each locomotive requiring its own traincrew, unless the second locomotive was being hauled 'dead' within the train consist. Here No 50 005 *Collingwood* heads No 47 111 at Liskeard with a train destined for the Midlands in the summer of 1975. *Author*

These two non-compatible locomotives, each of which can clearly be seen to have its own crew, were photographed at Saltash on 31 May 1973. Class 25 No 7677, the very last of 327 Class 25s to be built, and 'Western' No D1026 *Western Centurion*, are working in tandem as they pass the old goods yard with an up engineers' train of empty ballast hoppers. *G. F. Gillham*

Exhaust from two non-compatible locomotives is a tell-tale sign that both are under power, their drivers unleashing a total of over 5,000hp as they head the 07.40 Penzance–Liverpool away from Liskeard on 3 March 1984. No 47 488 leads No 50 031 *Hood* as the train crosses Bolitho Viaduct, hidden behind the trees, while in the distance (above the Class 47's cab) is Liskeard signalbox. *Author*

'Westerns' in Action

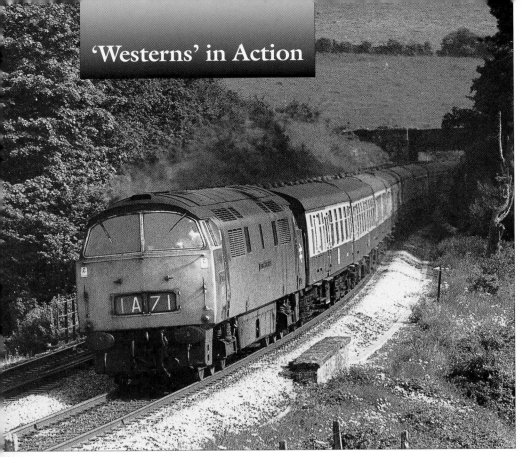

The 'Western' (later Class 52) diesel-hydraulics were the supreme motive power in the South West between 1962 and 1976, when Class 50s (themselves soon supplanted by IC125 units) took over the most prestigious expresses. Some would argue that the equally powerful Class 50s and the Sulzer-engined Class 45s and 47s were a match for the large diesel-hydraulics, but in terms of charisma, looks, sound and the size of their fan club the 'Westerns' undoubtedly 'ruled'. Taking a run at Dainton Bank with the 13.45 Penzance–Paddington on 4 June 1971 is No D1001 *Western Pathfinder. John Cooper-Smith*

Its number reflected in the headcode display, No D1051 *Western Ambassador* nears the summit of the climb to Burngullow on 19 May 1976 with the 10.55 Penzance–Paddington. The siding on the right (now lifted) was used to berth the up Sittingbourne clay-slurry tanker train. The line from here to Probus was eventually singled, but in 2004 double track was being reinstated, at considerable cost. *Author*

Headcode 6B64 relates to this Tavistock Junction–Exeter Riverside freight, seen passing the old wooden signalbox at Exminster on 16 July 1973 behind No D1057 *Western Chieftain*. The site of water troughs in steam days, Exminster station closed in 1964. The contract price for Class 52 construction was £115,000 per unit, but the final cost was slightly more, Crewe products costing marginally less than the Swindon-built machines. By 1964/5 some 25% of the class total fleet mileage was on freight workings, demonstrating a good mixed-traffic capability. *G. F. Gillham*

Late-afternoon sunshine backlights No D1032 *Western Marksman* on 6 August 1971 as it enters Newton Abbot with the 16.30 Plymouth–Paddington. The 'Westerns' had a 1,100gal fuel capacity and they carried 770 gallons of boiler water. *John Cooper-Smith*

Top left: Part of the present Gunnislake branch (prior to 1966 the Callington branch) between St Budeaux Victoria Road to Bere Alston was, until May 1968, the SR main line between Exeter and Plymouth. The original branch from Bere Alston to Callington did not open until 1908. Crossing the impressive Calstock Viaduct, which crosses the River Tamar separating Devon from Cornwall, on 23 April 1983 is the 11.30 Plymouth–Gunnislake, formed of two-car Class 118 DMU No P480. *Author*

Lower left: Well over 100ft high, Calstock Viaduct has 10 arches, each with a 60ft span, although it carries only a single track across the river. Crossing the imposing structure on 3 July 1981 was the experimental Class 140 diesel unit, No 140 001, forming the 14.45 special from Plymouth to Gunnislake. The four-wheeled carriages were based on bus bodies, and such trials influenced the eventual production of Class 142 and 143 units, which would feature briefly in the West Country later in the decade. *Author*

Right: This fascinating photograph, taken from the road bridge across the River Tamar using a high-powered Nikkor telephoto lens, shows two-car Class 118 DMU No P468 passing Ernesettle, on the Devon side of the river. On the right is the Ernesettle Ministry of Defence establishment, with a sprinkling of goods wagons on the standard-gauge sidings. The route was once double-track, but with only about eight round-trips per day by the branch DMU a single line is now adequate. *Author*

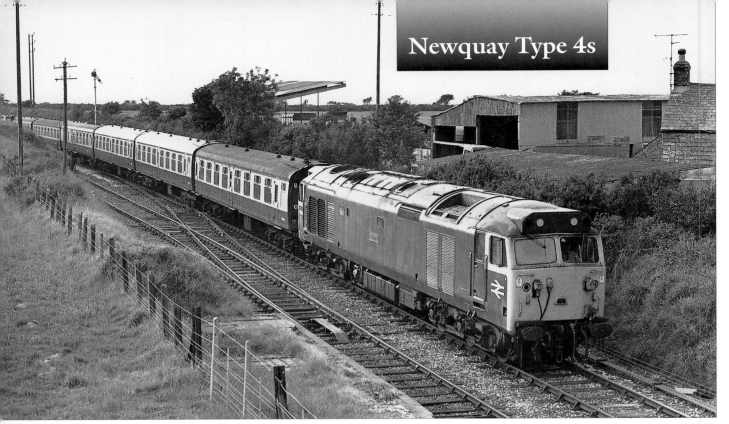

Newquay Type 4s

Once the single Saturdays-only through train from Falmouth to Paddington was withdrawn, in September 1979, the Newquay branch became the only survivor of the through-holiday-train phenomenon. The sight of full-length main-line Class 1 trains threading the sinuous 20¾-mile branch was (and still is) fascinating. No 50 049 *Defiance* rounds the curve approaching St Dennis Junction with an up train on 13 June 1980. *Author*

To commemorate the end of Class 52s in Cornwall the author organised the 'Western China Clay' Chartex for railway enthusiasts on 4 December 1976. The train travelled overnight from Paddington to Truro behind No D1023 *Western Fusilier* for a run over the Falmouth branch; No D1056 *Western Sultan* then worked to Par for a journey over the Newquay branch, becoming the last Class 52 to visit the terminus. On the return journey there was a photographic stop at Bugle: with all passengers back on board the train the special is about to depart for Lostwithiel. *Author*

Adding to the Type 4 variety on the Newquay branch on 2 July 1981 was this Class 47/0, seen passing Luxulyan with the 09.51 Newquay–Manchester. Over the years seasonal through trains, mostly on summer Saturdays, have run to a rich variety of destinations in the Midlands, the North of England and Scotland. Luxulyan once had a station building, an island platform loop, signalbox and sidings, but all were swept away in the 1960s, just a single-faced platform and a small waiting-hut surviving. *Author*

This was the view of the Newquay terminus in 1980 — a quarter of a century ago, at the time of writing. Although Newquay station had by this time already been 'rationalised', further changes would subsequently take place, including the abandonment (due to subsidence) of the platform occupied here by a 136-ton 1Co-Co1 'Peak'. In 1987 all sidings and run-round facilities were removed, along with the signalbox and all semaphore signals. The final indignity occurred in the 1990s, when the lovely old original (1876) station building was demolished to make way for a car park. The line is now a single-line stub from Goonbarrow Junction. *Author*

Above: The line from Waterloo to Exeter Central has become something of a secondary line, but back in the 1950s it was a faster route to the West Country than the GWR main line; in 1954 the best time from Paddington to Exeter St Davids was achieved by the 9.30am departure, which took 3 hours 10 minutes, whereas the 11am from Waterloo took 3 hours 5 minutes to Exeter Central. The best times in 2004 were 2 hours 3 minutes, with a single stop, via the former WR route by IC125 and 3 hours 1 minute, with 14 stops, on the old SR line, using Class 159 DMUs! Many trains on the SR continued to Exeter St Davids station, and this meant descending a 1-in-37 gradient. Pictured leaving St David's Tunnel and climbing into Central station is Class 33 No 33 048 with a through train to Brighton. *Author*

Below: The first of the SR's BRCW Type 3 (later Class 33) 'Cromptons' was delivered at the very end of 1959, and by June 1960 20 locomotives were in stock. These 1,550hp Bo-Bos were built by the Birmingham Railway Carriage & Wagon Co at Smethwick, the entire class of 98 being delivered by June 1962. In October 1971 the type took over Waterloo–Exeter workings from the 'Warships' of Classes 42 and 43. The normal headcode for the route was '62', but the infrequent services to Brighton displayed '11'. Services varied from year to year, but at times the Saturday train from Brighton loaded to 12 bogies, necessitating double-headed 'Cromptons'. Nos 33 058 and 33 026 are seen arriving at Exeter St Davids from the Sussex town in 1980. *Author*

By the late 1970s the Brighton–Exeter St Davids service ran only on Saturdays and for some time comprised an eight-coach 'Oxted' set of Mk 1 commuter stock, which was not required at weekends. Powering such a rake up through a closed and heavily 'rationalised' Seaton Junction is No 33 011. Once upon a time there were four tracks through this country junction! For some years there was a Fridays-only working from Brighton through to Penzance. *Author*

A dozen of the reliable BRCW Type 3s were built to narrow 'Hastings'-gauge body dimensions, being later known as Class 33/2s, while others were converted for push-pull working to operate the post-steam-era Bournemouth–Weymouth services with 'TC' stock, these being designated '33/1'. The proliferation of jumper cables was an easy means of identification, even if it did lead the less serious enthusiast to label the locomotives 'bagpipes'! Displaying the '11' headcode, this West Sussex Railway Touring Trust Chartex, organised by the author and his colleague Trevor Tupper for charitable purposes, leaves Dawlish on its way from Hove, Worthing and Chichester to Torquay and Paignton. *Author*

Diesel Drivers

Among the most neglected subjects in railway photography are railway employees, especially footplate crews. Driver Len Hooper of St Blazey was photographed at the controls of 'Warship' No D869 *Zest* at Newquay on 8 July 1962. His brother Albert was another well-known St Blazey driver who, sadly, is no longer with us. *M. Dart*

This anonymous old-timer is nearing the end of his career, but how refreshing to see somebody driving a 2,700hp Class 50 on the main line wearing a cloth cap! Quietly contemplating departure from Dawlish on the up line on 22 September 1984, he will soon be creating a considerable noise by opening the power handle of No 50 006 *Neptune. Author*

The author photographed Driver Prophet at Newquay from the footplate of No D1058 *Western Nobleman* on 6 August 1976. In those less formal days it was sometimes possible to scrounge a short cab ride, although the author would plead Not Guilty on this occasion! Note the single-line token for the run to St Dennis Junction. The driver is sporting a tie, thereby maintaining a long tradition for West Country drivers. *Author*

A New Approach

There is absolutely nothing wrong with conventional railway photography, where the train is taken 'three quarters on' at an approximately 45° angle. However, in any collection it is refreshing now and then to include something marginally more artistic. To guarantee dramatic lighting, which is so important to photography, it was necessary to be in position at 07.55 on a sunny April day to record this scene. A 200mm Nikon lens captures No 50 049 *Defiance* heading an empty-stock train westward past Liskeard signalbox. The backlighting highlights the signals and the ventilators on the carriage roofs. *Author*

A powerful shot recorded near Dawlish on 5 July 1979, skill and luck combining to produce a photograph with real impact. Perfectly framed by the short Kennaway Tunnel is Class 50 No 50 047 *Swiftsure* with an up train of 'Dogfish' ballast wagons. By chance a track worker with hammer over his shoulder is acknowledging an audible warning from the driver, adding human interest to the scene. *Brian Morrison*

With the sun sinking towards the horizon at the end of an April day in 1985, No 50 042 *Triumph* crosses the 150ft-high Moorswater Viaduct with a down express. Just below the viaduct was the English China Clay Moorswater drying plant, which would close in 1996. Happily freight activity recommenced in 1999, since when the site has been used as a cement-distribution centre. *Author*

Above: Yet again, lighting conditions convert a traditional photograph into something slightly different. Late in the day on 2 April 1979 the setting sun was not only backlighting these air-conditioned coaches but also highlighting the windows in the station overbridge at Bodmin Road. No 47 510 *Fair Rosamund* heads the 16.20 Penzance–Paddington. The foreground siding to the old goods yard has since been lifted. *Author*

Below: The conventional views of the South Devon sea wall between Dawlish Warren and Dawlish are relegated to the ordinary when compared with this striking view of No D1020 *Western Hero* heading the down 'Cornish Riviera' past Langstone Rock on 27 January 1971. It is the winter lighting that enhances the scene, combined with the dark (in shadow) framing of the shrubbery. The photographer duly became a very talented railway artist. *Philip D. Hawkins*

Of the many DMU classes the single cars produced by the Pressed Steel Co (later known as Class 121) and the Gloucester Railway Carriage & Wagon Co (Class 122) were arguably the most æsthetically pleasing, especially when working singly. In green livery with small yellow warning panel, Gloucester No W55000 waits at the pleasant terminus of Brixham with the 4.5pm to Churston on 4 May 1963. The branch line would close less than a fortnight later. *R. F. Roberts / Stephenson Locomotive Society*

A wide-angle lens was necessary to secure this shot at St Erth of the St Ives 'bubble car'. On 9 November 1985 Class 121 car No W55033 awaits a main-line connection before departing for the attractive resort on the North Cornwall coast. In the summer months a Park & Ride service was introduced, whereby motorists parked their cars at the nearby Lelant Saltings and travelled into the congested holiday resort by train. *Author*

The Looe-branch platform at Liskeard is set at right-angles to the main line. Under the GWR station awning unit No P125 (Plymouth-allocated Class 121 car No W55025) waits in the darkness to depart with the 18.25 for Looe on 19 February 1982. After dark branch trains do not stop at the intermediate stations, due to the absence of platform lighting. *Author*

Magnificent Cornwall in the late afternoon of an October day finds Class 122 'bubble car' No 55012 about to cross the River Lynher with the 15.54 Plymouth–Liskeard local. These single cars had two 150hp engines and weighed between 35 and 37 tons, giving an impressive power-to-weight ratio; seating was provided for 65 passengers. *Author*

Passing 'Peaks'

Above: Some might say that photographing passing trains doubles the interest, and this spread features Class 45 and 46 'Peaks' passing other types of motive power. In the first photograph, taken on 23 April 1975, Class 45/0 No 45 023 *Royal Pioneer Corps* leaves Penzance with the 14.00 for Bristol Temple Meads, passing Class 25 No 25 326 stabled in the down sidings with a Mk 2b coach. *Brian Morrison*

Below: Another drab day in Cornwall, with further time spent sheltering under St Austell station's awnings, was rewarded by an unidentified Class 46 on a down train passing a tired-looking Class 50, No 50 019 with an up express for Paddington. On 19 May 1976 the Class 50 had yet to be named, while refurbishment was merely a glint in the WR Locomotive Development Engineer's eye. *Author*

A busy scene at Par, the junction station for Newquay, in February 1984. Appearing on a local Plymouth–Penzance train is a Class 45/0, its steam-heating boiler providing some comfort for passengers. In the meantime the station awnings reverberate to the sound being emitted from the four exhaust ports of the 16-cylinder English Electric engine of Class 50 No 50 006 *Neptune*, vigorously departing with an up local from Penzance. *Author*

Nearly 68ft in length, powered by a 2,500hp 12-cylinder Sulzer 12LDA28B diesel engine and featuring Brush electrical equipment, the design known later as the Class 46 was introduced in 1961.
This particular locomotive, No 46 025, was new (as No D162) in April 1962 and would be withdrawn in December 1980; on 16 September 1979 it was heading a down train at Lostwithiel when Class 50 No 50 008 *Thunderer* appeared on the up road with a Paddington-bound express. *Author*

Torbay

Left: On the railway map the line from Aller Junction to Torquay, Paignton and Kingswear appears as a branch (and, indeed, the line originally ran only as far as Torre), but over the years the Torbay area has been the destination for Class 1 and 2 trains from many corners of the British mainland. Passing Torquay Gas Works, which once boasted its own sidings (note the goods wagons in the left background), on 2 August 1961 is NBL Type 2 No D6333 with a Manchester–Kingswear train. *Ian G. Holt*

Below: Passing the same location as that depicted in the previous photograph (but over four years later, on 4 September 1965) is the down 'Torbay Express' (10.30 ex Paddington), entrusted to No D1048 *Western Lady.* The locomotive is in maroon livery — a fitting match to the rake of (mostly) Mk 1 coaches. *Western Lady* would survive until the very last day of the 'Westerns' (26 February 1977), hauling the last-ever privately sponsored railtour, organised by the author — the 'Western Lament', which ran from Paddington to Castle Cary, unusually on a Thursday, 24 February 1977. *A. N. Yeates*

Right: The double crossover in the foreground leads the eye to the oncoming train — the 10.18 Paddington–Paignton, powered by No 50 038 *Formidable* — passing Paignton's home signals on 14 September 1985. There seem to be some 'bellowers' on board who are appreciating Class 50 haulage. The covered colour light (beside the third coach) would soon sound the death-knell for the old semaphore signals. *Author*

Cowley Bridge

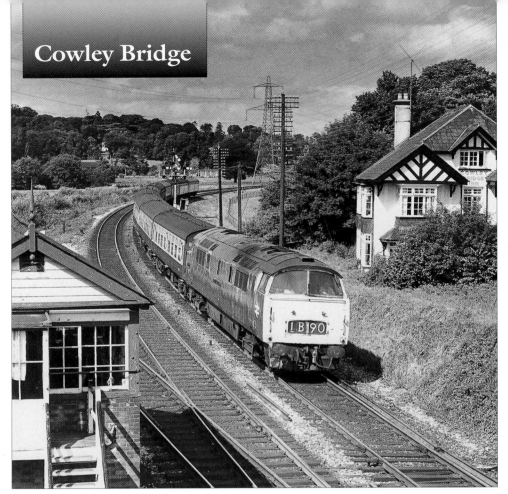

Cowley Bridge Junction, just north of Exeter St Davids, is where the line to Barnstaple and Okehampton leaves the GWR main line to Taunton. In days of old the lines on the left comprised the LSWR/SR route(s) that served Ilfracombe via Barnstaple and Plymouth via Okehampton and Tavistock. Passing the half-timbered Cowley Bridge Inn on a glorious 19 July 1973 is No D1072 *Western Glory* with the 13.30 Paddington–Penzance. *John Cooper-Smith*

In the late 1970s the 'feed' onto the main line was singled, and as a result trains to Exeter had briefly to run 'wrong line' past Cowley Bridge Junction signalbox. After the replacement of Class 25s in the West Country (by Class 37s in 1979/80) certain trains between Exeter and Barnstaple were hauled by SR-based Class 33 'Cromptons'; on 18 August 1984 No 33 014 joins the main line with the 14.10 from Barnstaple. *David Brown*

Brake-van Lament

Above: The humble brake van was a vital part of old-fashioned unfitted goods trains. On downhill sections the guard would turn the large brake wheel inside the van to keep couplings taut. The van was also used in shunting operations and provided a weather-proof 'home' for the train guard and sometimes a shunter. The brake van is much loved by railway modellers, and by chance an 'N'-gauge proprietary model of this Class 08, No 08 113, was marketed a few years ago. After working to Wenford Bridge the delightful little train passes Treesmill on its way back to St Blazey from Bodmin Road on 23 July 1982. *Author*

Below: A sight that has gone forever is the working from ECC's Ponts Mill china-clay works, now closed and demolished. Trundling the rural branch freight, comprising just two wagons and a brake van, towards the junction with the Newquay branch on 4 May 1989 is No 08 955. The wagons will travel all the way to Fort William in Scotland, and the china clay within will be used in the paper-making process. The last china-clay train left Ponts Mill on 21 April 1992. *Author*

Penzance MPD

Left: It is not clear to all railway enthusiasts that, although prior to 1914 the engine shed at Penzance was near the station, from that date the MPD was located some distance away from the terminus, at Long Rock. In later years sidings adjacent to the station became a locomotive-stabling point, but visiting diesel locomotives continued to use the old steam shed, and it was not until 1980 that a brand-new depot was opened and new sidings for IC125 sets were provided. Here No 50 017 *Royal Oak* shelters in the new depot at Long Rock on 12 June 1981. *Author*

Below: The tracks at Long Rock and adjacent Ponsandane were multi-purpose, being used for stock stabling and as a general goods yard. Once coal traffic ceased the only commodity handled was fuel for BR's own diesel locomotives and units. Pictured outside the old Long Rock shed on 6 August 1976 is Class 52 No D1058 *Western Nobleman*, which had worked down overnight with the 23.35 Paddington–Penzance. *Author*

Right: Although steam in Cornwall effectively finished in 1962, some 12 years later — on 22 June 1974 — the remains of the old coaling stage and water tower at the erstwhile Penzance MPD at Long Rock were still *in situ*, albeit in dilapidated condition. Framed in a broken window, which adds hugely to the sense of dereliction, is No D1036 *Western Emperor*. *Philip D. Hawkins*

'Warships' at Aller Junction

Above: Aller Junction was always a favourite with railway photographers, being not only the point where the Plymouth and Paignton lines diverge but also graced by a couple of overbridges that afforded excellent views of trains in both directions. Here, on 14 July 1971, Class 43 'Warship' No 853 *Thruster* heads the 16.30 Paddington–Penzance; with a 10-coach load the 2,200hp NBL machine will have its work cut out on the 1-in-37 climb to Dainton Tunnel. *G. F. Gillham*

Below: By 22 July 1972 only 12 of the 71 B-B 'Warships' (Classes 42 and 43) were left in service, and by the end of the year the entire fleet would be extinct in BR service. In such circumstances the photographer was no doubt pleased to record No 805 *Benbow* approaching Aller Junction with the 12.26SO Paddington–Penzance. *G. F. Gillham*

Above: The NBL/MAN-engined Class 43s were generally regarded as being less successful than their Maybach-engined sister locomotives. Transmissions were also different, the Class 43 having Voith equipment and the Class 42 Mekydro. On 14 July 1969 the signal is 'off' on the down Plymouth line at Aller Junction for Class 43 No D845 *Sprightly*, which will have trouble living up to its name with a motley collection of speed-restricted ballast wagons in tow! *G. F. Gillham*

Below: Rounding off a quartet of Geoff Gillham's excellent photographs is this view of blue-liveried Class 42 No 868 *Zephyr* with a long Class 6 train of 25 four-wheeled box vans on 21 July 1970. Class 42s were numbered from D800 to D832 and from D866 to D870, whereas Class 43s were numbered from D833 to D865. Fortunately two of the former avoided the cutter's torch and survive in preservation, but the NBL Class 43s are truly extinct. *G. F. Gillham*

Above: The arrival of the 1,750hp Class 37s in Devon and Cornwall was a revelation. Not only did these 105-ton locomotives have considerably more horsepower and traction than the Class 25s, but they were also 'top of the pops' in terms of reliability/availability figures. The first arrived in the South West in 1979, and gradually the number increased. One, No 37 207, was eventually named *William Cookworthy*, honouring the apothecary credited with discovering china clay in Cornwall. On the pleasant afternoon of 19 April 1985 'Cookers' passes Restormel, near Lostwithiel, with cement tankers for Chacewater. This traffic would cease in 1987. *Author*

Below: Although St Blazey station — known prior to 1878 as Par (CMR) station — was closed in 1925 (albeit used for workmen's trains until 1934) the platforms are still largely intact. On 16 June 1982 No 37 207 *William Cookworthy*, having just run down the spur from Par station on the main line with a couple of engineers wagons, has come to a halt at the old station and will now reverse into St Blazey Yard. The signalman has already given the train the road. *Author*

If you stand on Cornish overbridges for long enough train crews will eventually recognise you, hence the 'thumbs up' from the driver of No 37 271. With windscreen wipers flailing against the driving rain, he probably thinks the photographer has just escaped from an institution. With nearly 50 empty clay hoods in tow the 'Siphon' is passing Treesmill *en route* for St Blazey Yard on 4 June 1981. *Author*

This curious road bridge is at Coombe Junction, near Liskeard. In the 19th century the left-hand arch was for the railway line from Moorswater to Looe and that on the right was for the old Liskeard & Looe Union Canal. Trains still run under the bridge to visit the distribution depot at Moorswater, but nowadays the traffic is inbound cement rather than outbound china clay. With driver and shunter in evidence No 37 135 awaits the 'right away' for the run up to Liskeard with loaded clay hoods on 22 February 1982. *Author*

The Torrington Line

Above: Passenger trains served Torrington from Halwill Junction until 1 March 1965 and from the Barnstaple Junction direction until 4 October 1965. From the end of the year the lines were used only for freight traffic, milk and ball clay being the principal commodities, general goods facilities having been withdrawn with effect from 6 September 1965. With just a brake van in tow, Class 22 No D6339 arrives at Torrington to collect some milk wagons on 22 July 1970. The museum-piece of a signal on the left is a surviving LSWR lower-quadrant example! *G. F. Gillham*

Below: After closure to passengers part of the old North Devon & Cornwall Junction Light Railway from Halwill Junction to Torrington continued to be used for ball-clay traffic, such trains working to Meeth, where there was a sizeable clay works. On its way to Torrington, Barnstaple and Exeter on 22 July 1970, Class 22 No D6333 rounds a tight curve, with checkrail in place, near the tiny station of Watergate. *G. F. Gillham*

Above: Earlier the same day the photographer captured No D6333 on its outward journey to ECC Meeth with just four empty wagons and a brake van, this time passing the weed-covered platforms of the old Petrockstow station, where there was a passing-loop. The train had just climbed a 1-in-50 gradient, just discernible in the background. These locomotives were called 'Baby Warships' because their 1,100hp NBL/MAN diesel engines were almost identical to (but not interchangeable with) the engines used in pairs in the Class 43 'Warships'. *G. F. Gillham*

Below: In the days of passenger trains the old ND&CJLR line had only two trains per day in each direction, with an equal number of freights over its northern section. Just south of Dunsbear Halt, seen here, were the sidings of the North Devon Clay Co's Marland Works, and clay workers who lived near Torrington used the halt in considerable numbers. In this cracking shot No D6334 and 10 tarpaulin-covered ball-clay wagons plus a brake van pass Dunsbear Halt on their way to Torrington and beyond. *Ian Allan Library*

The very last train to Torrington was a truly spectacular affair. On 6 November 1982 a train comprising 15 coaches with nearly 850 rail fans on board traversed the branch behind two 1,470hp Class 31s, with a locomotive at each end due to the train's length, which precluded running round. With hundreds of enthusiasts swarming on the platform, No 31 174 is seen adorned with floral wreath and home-made 'Last Atlantic Coast Express' headboard; sister locomotive No 31 158 was at the far end of the train. The fertiliser depot on the right was built on the site once occupied by the lovely old stone goods shed. The tracks would be lifted in 1984. *Author*

The Ilfracombe Branch

Top right: Another former SR line from Barnstaple Junction continued through Braunton to Ilfracombe. During the diesel era passenger trains could be worked by Classes 22, 35 and 42/43, as well as an assortment of DMUs. On 1 September 1965 it was the turn of 'Hymek' (Class 35) No D7068 to traverse the Ilfracombe line with a five-coach train from Exeter to Ilfracombe, seen here ascending Mortehoe Bank. Once upon a time the line was busy enough to justify double track. *P. H. Wells*

Lower right: The Ilfracombe–Barnstaple Junction line closed on 5 October 1970, and what was probably the last locomotive-hauled train over the branch (and almost certainly the last to be double-headed) was a West Sussex Railway Touring Trust Chartex from Sussex. Run on Sunday 30 August 1970, the 'Atlantic Coast Limited' most unusually brought to the line a pair of Class 33 'Cromptons', including No D6566 (later No 33 048). Seen from the buffer stops under the overall roof at Ilfracombe, excursionists make for the town and the sea. *Author*

Below: Trains running from Barnstaple Junction to Barnstaple Town station, where the famous narrow-gauge Lynton & Barnstaple Railway operated, had to cross the River Taw by this fragile-looking single-track bridge. It is hard to imagine that 'West Country' Pacifics worked over the bridge with a portion of the 'Atlantic Coast Express'! A rather more mundane sight, but one that would be welcome today, is No D6334 with an Ilfracombe–Exeter St Davids train on 2 September 1965. The SR utility van behind the locomotive is a nice touch and provides a link with the former 'owners'. *P. H. Wells*

Although it is always the main-line diesels that attract publicity and receive the adoration of the fans, until very recent times it was the humble Class 08 shunter that assembled freight trains and worked the most minor lines and sidings. One of the places where the 0-6-0s are still active is Fowey Docks at Carne Point, south of Lostwithiel, seen here. Coupled to its match wagon, the 'Grunt' toys with a single clay hood on the private riverside sidings, owned by the English China Clay Co (since taken over by French company Imerys). *Author*

One of the most fascinating lengths of track in Cornwall was the crossing at the tiny hamlet of Helland, on the Boscarne Junction–Wenford Bridge line. With driver Albert Hooper leaning out of his cab and shunter Bill Richards having a quick scowl from the brake van, the returning Wenford goods squeezes between cottages on 14 June 1978, Class 08 No 08 091 providing the motive power. The trackbed here is now part of the Camel Trail footpath/cycleway. *Author*

There are no prizes for guessing what the weather was doing on this day in May 1976! In the days when there was an active (albeit hardly lucrative) railway parcels business St Austell station was something of a focal point for this part of southern Cornwall. A Class 08, fitted with an English Electric 350hp six-cylinder engine, arrives at the down platform with a GUV and three utility vans, while in the down siding (long since lifted) is another van. The station buildings on the down side have since been demolished and replaced by a modern structure. *Author*

A regular haunt for Class 08 diesel shunters in Cornwall was the clay works at Ponts Mill, at the end of a long siding off the Newquay branch, to the north of St Blazey Gate. The train normally ran once per day unless the wagons had to be left for loading, in which case two round trips between Ponts Mill and St Blazey yard were made. Being drawn out of the works by No 08 955 on 24 January 1991 are two 80-ton 'Tiger' bogie wagons containing powdered china clay destined for Mossend in Scotland. Note the weed-covered track on this pleasant byway. *Author*

1Co-Co1 Freight

Having just crossed from Somerset into the county of Devon an unidentified Class 45/0 with split headcode panel leaves Whiteball Tunnel, the summit of the climb from Wellington, with a mixed rake of older-style vacuum-braked wagons on 30 June 1979. The semaphore signals were controlled by the diminutive Whiteball signalbox, located just beyond the field of view on the down side. The train is travelling from Bristol East Yard to Exeter Riverside. *Author*

They certainly don't make them like this anymore! A truly period freight of more than 45 four-wheeled wagons, with a traditional brake van bringing up the rear, has left Burslecombe behind and is approaching Whiteball Summit in the late spring of 1980. Although the nominal maximum speed of the 'Peak' classes was 90mph Class 45/0 No 45 024 would be running at little more than 45mph because of the speed restrictions placed on these elderly wagons and the 1-in-115 gradient at this point. *Author*

Above: Although it is risky to make a definitive statement it would appear that the first Class 46 foray into Cornwall was on 30 December 1969, and by January 1970 several of the class were noted in the Plymouth area. Laira depot eventually had an allocation of Class 46s for several years. Having worked the Chacewater cement train down from Tavistock Junction on 10 June 1980, Class 46 No 46 002 had to continue to Drump Lane, Redruth, in order to run round. Here the return train passes Drump Lane signalbox before crossing from the down to the up main line. *Author*

Below: A train from the Heathfield branch, near Newton Abbot, arrives at Lostwithiel on 2 April 1979 behind Class 46 No 46 015. A thin yellow band at the base of the tarpaulins over the wagons indicates that the load is ball clay (rather than china clay), which will be tripped down to Carne Point, Fowey, for shipment. At this time the original Cornwall Railway station was still hanging on by a thread, but the demolition contractors would eventually win the day. *Author*

St Blazey by Night and Day

Left: Erected in 1873/4 to unique design, St Blazey depot was built in brick on the roundhouse-and-turntable principle, with nine bays, each capable of holding two small Cornwall Minerals Railway tank locomotives — or a single Class 50! The depot continued to operate thus for 114 years, until 24 April 1987. Late in the evening of 18 February 1982 the roundhouse looks full, 'Hoovers' Nos 50 012 *Benbow* and 50 045 *Achilles* being sandwiched between Class 37 No 37 135 and Class 47 No 47 358. *Author*

Below: Evening at St Blazey on 18 February 1982 finds 136-ton Class 45 'Peak' No 45 002 looking slightly gaunt in the available winter light. The type had a three-piece windscreen, unbelievably small buffers and a short nose that produced a distinctive appearance. Prominent just below the BR logo is the sanding box, used to aid adhesion when starting or on slippery rails. *Author*

Right: 'Tis rainin' again, with droplets literally bouncing off the roof of Class 47/0 No 47 089 *Amazon* at a damp St Blazey on 2 October 1985. The lines in the foreground are radiating from the turntable. Note the huge doors, which could be closed once locomotives had been berthed in the brick building. In the days of steam St Blazey was designated '83E', and in diesel days locomotives based there carried a 'BZ' sticker. However, in today's train-operating environment locomotives belong to a 'pool' and travel the country like nomads. *Author*

The Climb

Although IC125 units and 'Voyagers' have so much power available that drivers have actually to ease the power handle over the South Devon banks, in the past the climb to Dainton Tunnel was a severe test for steam locomotives and demanding for diesels. With both Maybach engines humming No D1040 *Western Queen* gets to grips with the 1-in-37 climb with the 16.30 Paddington–Penzance on 7 July 1974. *G. F. Gillham*

Absolutely blasting out of the tunnel on full power and surrounded by a haze of exhaust from the 24 Maybach cylinders, No D1040 *Western Queen* features again but this time on train 1A45, the 12.55pm Penzance–Paddington, on 6 August 1971. At this point the train would be travelling at barely 30mph, although within a few yards it will be 'power off' for the descent towards Aller Junction. *John Cooper-Smith*

With the delightful Devon hills in the background, train 1B25, the 11-coach 8.30am Paddington–Penzance, nears Dainton Summit behind No D1001 *Western Pathfinder* on 6 August 1971. The ancient sign on the left states that 'ALL UP GOODS AND MINERAL TRAINS MUST STOP DEAD HERE'. This was so the train guard could 'pin down' the brakes for the 1-in-37 descent towards Stoneycombe Quarry, thereby preventing runaways, but with the advent of the continuous brake and fully fitted trains such signs have become redundant. *John Cooper-Smith*

What a lovely way to spend an evening! Towards the end of a summer's day and with the sun developing a warm tone, the 12-coach 1V93 10.06 Edinburgh–Plymouth winds its way through the curves on the approach to Dainton Tunnel behind Class 47 No 1989 (later No 47 287). The yellow and black lower quadrant distant signal is 'off' for an up train. The photograph was taken on 20 July 1973. *G. F. Gillham*

Above: Cornwall has had a long history of van trains that included postal, parcels, perishables and newspaper workings. As late as the 1970s and 1980s van trains to Glasgow, Bristol, Paddington and even Redhill worked up from Penzance during daylight hours. Squashed flies aside, No 50 035 *Ark Royal* was in immaculate condition as it headed the heavy 12.10 Penzance–Glasgow parcels past Carlyon Bay, west of Par, on 2 June 1981. *Author*

Below: Most parcel workings stopped for loading at major stations such as Truro and St Austell. At the latter location lines of Royal Mail vans would queue up so that parcels could be transferred from road to rail — a source of traffic that would be lost at the beginning of 2004. On 22 February 1982 No 50 026 *Indomitable* hauls the 12.10 Penzance–Glasgow vans out of St Austell while on the right an ancient GWR sign warns the public not to trespass on railway property. *Author*

On 9 June 1980 No 50 046 *Ajax* had been named but not refurbished as it headed the 14.50 Penzance–Paddington perishables between Dobwalls and Liskeard. The old four-wheeled wooden-bodied SR utility vans, such as that behind the locomotive, were restricted to 60mph, and this had to be taken into consideration when train pathing was being considered. *Author*

The Bristol van train was normally shorter than either the Paddington or the Glasgow train but stopped at Plymouth, where additional vans were added. Passing mature rhododendron shrubs on the approach to the closed Chacewater station on 12 June 1980 is No 50 045 *Achilles*. In years gone by there was a third track at this location, used by branch trains travelling to/from Newquay via Perranporth. *Author*

Skirting Exmoor

The Taunton–Barnstaple (Victoria) line started in Somerset, entered the County of Devon at Venn Cross and then re-entered Somerset at Dulverton, only to pass into Devon again at East Anstey, *en route* passing along the southern edge of Exmoor and through some attractive scenery. In this most unusual picture NBL Type 2 No D6336 heads a special train carrying the world-famous 'Beatles' pop group, seen passing Bishops Nympton & Molland on its return trip from South Molton. The leafless trees and the steam leaking from the steam pipes tend to confirm the date as 6 March, but the photographer did not record the year, which is believed to have been 1964. *John Spencer Gilks*

One of only three photographs in *Diesel Days: Devon and Cornwall* that was not taken in either county. However, Dulverton, in Somerset, is only just over the border from Devon and had significant links with that county, such as being the junction station for the Exe Valley branch to Exeter. The line closed on 1 October 1966, and on the last day trains were strengthened to cope with the crowds. Here the five-car 13.28 from Taunton to Barnstaple, formed of a two-car Pressed Steel and a three-car Swindon 'Cross-Country DMU, is seen at the rural and somewhat dilapidated station on the last day of service. *Author*

The Specials

Although in March 1970 two pairs of SR Class 33s had worked special trains to St Germans, with the stock travelling further west, 'Cromptons' were a rarity in Cornwall. It was therefore not surprising that the Railway Pictorial Publications Railtours (RPPR) 'Deltic to Devon/Cromptons to Cornwall' tour of 16 October 1977 was full to the brim. The 'Deltic' failed to materialise because of an(other) ASLEF dispute, but a pair of Class 40s provided an interesting substitute as far as Newton Abbot, where 'Cromptons' took over. Leaving Par to pull up the stock are Nos 33 017 and 33 022. *Author*

Many of the freight-only branch lines in Devon and Cornwall were regular targets for the organisers of enthusiasts' railtours, and on this occasion it was the turn of Pathfinder Tours, run by the author's old colleague Peter Watts. The tour included the remains of the old Moretonhampstead branch (by then the Heathfield branch and used for oil and clay traffic) in one of his itineraries.
With a pixie on its lamp bracket a Class 37 runs round the stock at Heathfield while the shunter holds the tail lamp in one hand and the single-line token (which he is about to surrender to the driver) in the other. The branch curving away to the right was the old Teign Valley line to Exeter, which closed to passengers in June 1958 but which remained open for goods to Trusham for a while. *Author*

Top left: The last Class 52s ever to traverse the Falmouth branch were No D1023 *Western Fusilier*, seen here, and D1056 *Western Sultan*, at the other end of the train. The 'Western China Clay' had worked down from Paddington overnight on 3/4 December 1976, and the Chartex would later visit Newquay and Carne Point, Fowey. The locomotive's steam-heating boiler is working well, but the steam pipes between the carriages seem to have had their day and are leaking profusely. *Author*

Top right: One of the most prestigious specials to travel into Cornwall was the RPPR 'Penzance Pullman' of 26 April 1980, which comprised eight First-class Mk 1 coaches and four restaurant cars, the catering vehicles being evenly distributed throughout the train, *i.e.* between every two coaches — a shunter's nightmare! Although the train visited Penzance there was an additional run from Par to St Dennis Junction and back. Here Nos 25 155 and 37 299 cross over from the down main line to the Newquay branch at Par on the down run. The two classes both had 'blue star' coupling codes and could be worked in multiple with a single crew. Note the tablecloth being hung out to dry on the leading restaurant car! *John Chalcraft*

Lower left: After running well over 40 railtours between 1976 and 1980 RPPR ceased operations due to substantial increases in train-charter rates charged by BR. The very last tour was the 'Mayflower', on 12 October 1980, which was locomotive-hauled from Paddington to Plymouth, a DMU formation being used over Devon and Cornwall branch lines. Here Class 118 unit No P480 curves away from the main line at Liskeard and takes the spur to the Looe-branch platform. No passengers were allowed on the train for this movement. The DMU went on to visit Moorswater and other freight-only lines. *Author*

Right: A record photograph included merely to show the very unusual sight of a pair of ER Class 40s at Newton Abbot on the 'Deltics to Devon/Cromptons to Cornwall' RPPR railtour of 16 October 1977. Seen ready to depart with the return journey to Paddington, Nos 40 083 and 40 081 have both been blowing out coolant, judging by the stains on the body sides. *Author*

Lower right: Meldon Quarry is the venue for this 'seminar' shot on the 'Westerns South Western' railtour of 30 October 1976, featuring 'Westerns' Nos D1023 *Western Fusilier* and D1009 *Western Invader*. Amongst the crowd are Chris Broadhurst and Keith Gloster (headboard makers), Chris Guntripp, Tony Alosko, Steve Chandler and 'Fidel' (BR employees), a grinning author and organiser (with badge and tie!) and Colin Marsden, immediately on his left, who 26 years later would become Editor of *Railways Illustrated*. It is sobering to think that these youngsters will now all be men in their 40s, 50s and — dare one say — 60s! *Norman E. Preedy*

There is something fascinating about branch lines, especially when a Class 08 is passing long-closed platforms with just a single wagon. The line to Marsh Mills from Tavistock Junction (Plymouth) is still in operation for china-clay movements. It is also the home of the Plym Valley Railway, based on the old GWR branch to Tavistock. On 18 May 1984 No 08 953 passes the remains of Marsh Mills station, closed on 31 December 1962, and makes for Tavistock Junction with a single 80-tonne 'Tiger' wagon. *Author*

Something of a forgotten corner of Plymouth is the line from Plymouth Friary and the Laira area down to Cattewater (see the 'Small Shunters' section). Passing some ancient and dilapidated industrial architecture on 10 August 1984 is No 08 792, returning from Cattewater with a rake of tank wagons. *Rod Muncey*

'50s' in the Landscape

A Class 50 was first noted at Plymouth Laira depot in November 1973, and from that time the class was gradually transferred to the WR from the LMR, so that by May 1976 all fifty Class 50s were allocated to the WR. They were soon at work on all types of train as the remaining diesel-hydraulics were gradually withdrawn. Looking well-travelled and work-stained, No 50 006 *Neptune* leaves Par with a St Blazey–Tavistock Junction freight on 17 April 1985. This had been the first Class 50 to be refurbished and would be the second to be withdrawn from service, on 1 July 1987. *Author*

Above: The railway photographer must be 'up with the lark' to take an action photograph of the overnight Paddington–Penzance sleeping-car train. There were always a few normal coaches on the back for 'wakers', but behind the BG van the following four vehicles are distinctive Mk 1 sleeping cars. Approaching Marazion early on the morning of 7 June 1980 is No 50 010 *Monarch. Author*

Below: One of the finer landscapes in Cornwall is the valley of the River Fowey just below Restormel Castle, visible above the cab of the locomotive. A golf course has now been built on both sides of the line at this point. The Lostwithiel signalman is aware of this down train on 2 March 1984 and has pulled off his outer home signal as No 50 004 *St Vincent* slows for its station stop. The small signal on the right is for the down goods loop. *Author*

Right: All along the south side of the Glynn and Fowey valleys there has been massive investment in forestry, and fast-growing conifers have been planted on the hillsides, changing the landscape for many decades to come. Two other notable features of the Cornish railway landscape are stone bridges (constructed using a plentiful local resource) and, at a decreasing number of locations, lower-quadrant semaphore signals. All of these ingredients are present in this photograph of No 50 033 *Glorious* approaching Lostwithiel with a down train. Note the slip point protecting the up main from the up loop. *Author*

277

In the glorious era when most local stopping trains between Penzance and Plymouth comprised locomotives and stock (as distinct from multiple-units) No 50 047 *Swiftsure* crosses the 297ft-long, 52ft-high Chacewater Viaduct on 14 October 1982 with an up working comprising three coaches and a BG van. There is now no station between Redruth and Truro, Scorrier and Chacewater both having closed in October 1964. *Author*

A coastal landscape at Carlyon Bay, where the railway runs through a golf course located on top of the cliffs fronting the beach. A distinctive train of the era was the Kensington Olympia–St Austell Motorail, which normally comprised eight Mk 1 coaches for car drivers and their passengers and eight or nine low-loaders that carried their cars. This traffic was never properly developed, and after separating the drivers from their cars by running two separate trains and substantially increasing transportation rates and fares, BR withdrew the service altogether. On 7 June 1980 No 50 046 *Ajax* was in charge of the SO working, which operated only from the end of May until mid-September. For many years there was also a thrice-weekly Motorail service between Newton Abbot and Inverness! *Author*

In retrospect Class 31s in Devon were never rare, but neither were they particularly numerous. However, they were seen more regularly in the county from 1976. For many years the early-morning Plymouth–Old Oak Common vans produced an example, and this resulted in daily appearances through Exeter St Davids. Some of the class found themselves on the stabling-point at Exeter, and they were often drafted into service on local trains to Newton Abbot and Paignton. In Class 1 terms the class's main claim to fame was its operation of the SO through train from Paddington to Barnstaple. In May 1980 Nos 31 210 and 31 286 wait to leave Exeter St Davids station for Paddington with such a train. *Author*

Exeter '31s'

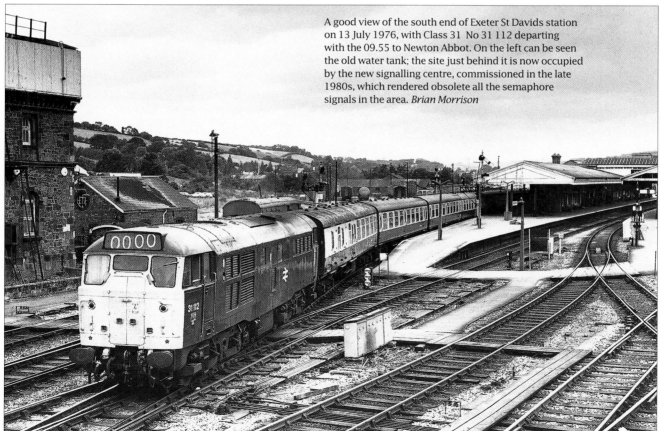

A good view of the south end of Exeter St Davids station on 13 July 1976, with Class 31 No 31 112 departing with the 09.55 to Newton Abbot. On the left can be seen the old water tank; the site just behind it is now occupied by the new signalling centre, commissioned in the late 1980s, which rendered obsolete all the semaphore signals in the area. *Brian Morrison*

Above: These photographs show the popular Class 37s on Cornish branch lines, most of which are open only for the transportation of china clay. Passing an old fixed distant signal on the banks of the River Fowey, just south of Lostwithiel, on 10 August 1983 is No 37 270, heading for Carne Point, Fowey, with loaded clay hoods. With 1,750hp available and six-wheeled bogies the Class 37s were ideally suited to the task and represented a significant improvement over both the Class 22 diesel-hydraulics and the Class 25 diesel-electrics. *Author*

Below: Despite their Type 3 power output the Class 37s occasionally worked double-headed, particularly on the heaviest trains serving ECC Rocks at Goonbarrow Junction. Rolling along the largely level Fowey branch on 16 April 1985 are Nos 37 181 and 37 247 with a massive 56-wagon train bound initially for Lostwithiel, where the train will reverse before continuing to Par, Luxulyan and Goonbarrow. *Author*

Above: An interesting load over the years has been the transportation of china clay in these large (80-tonne) 'Polybulk' wagons bound for destinations on the European mainland, particularly in Switzerland and Italy. Leaving the sidings at Goonbarrow Junction for St Blazey on 9 June 1980 is No 37 299, as a DMU scuttles towards Newquay. With the departure of the DMU the single line to St Blazey will now be clear for the clay train. *Author*

Below: Having reversed at Lostwithiel, this long train of empty clay hoods is approaching St Blazey Gate on the Newquay branch on its way to ECC Rocks at Goonbarrow. The train was photographed on 15 April 1985, during a week when Nos 37 181 and 37 247 worked in multiple on a daily basis. In days gone by the water in streams such as this was white in colour from china-clay workings, but efforts were made over the years by ECC to clean up its act, and in this it was hugely successful. *Author*

Above: The rarely photographed china-clay 'dries' at Treviscoe on 19 February 1982 finds No 37 135 indulging in a little shunting activity. The 'main' branch to Parkandillack is on the left, and except for the connecting spur the track in the works area is set in concrete. The works adjoins Kernick clay 'dries', and both continue to be rail-served in the new millennium. The train will soon continue along the branch to Drinnick Mill and Burngullow. *Author*

Below: Over the years the massive conical clay tips have been somewhat levelled, in common with many slag heaps at coal mines. An example is this tip by the former West of England China Clay Works, near Drinnick Mill. Descending from Lukes Old siding in April 1985, this brace of Class 37s will call briefly at Drinnick Mill goods office, where shunter Ivor Trudgeon will alight and deal with the paperwork. Although the Class 37s were at home in Cornwall they did experience considerable wheel-flange wear on the tight curves in clay works. *Author*

Single-track Main Line

During 1964 the impressive St Pinnock and Largin viaducts were beginning to feel their age, and a vast amount of money was required to maintain their double-track main-line status. Instead of undertaking strengthening works the authorities decided to single a short section of the main line. This section of track was under the control of Largin signalbox. The staccato booming of 16 cylinders of English Electric engine reverberating off the hillside is almost audible as No 50 033 *Glorious* leaves Largin Viaduct and pounds up the 1-in-58 climb to Doublebois with the 07.40 Penzance–Liverpool on 10 August 1983. A 200mm Nikkor lens captures the exhaust haze and the curving nature of the track alignment at this point in the Glynn Valley. *Author*

Devon 'Cromptons'

As already mentioned the Class 33 'Cromptons' (the nickname originating from their Crompton-Parkinson traction motors) took over the Waterloo–Exeter services from the Class 42 and 43 'Warships' in October 1971. With only 1,550hp available (a little over 1,200hp at the rail) the small Type 3s had to work hard over the years, especially as most trains over the route stopped at all stations. Trains normally loaded to eight coaches, but often nine-coach rakes were provided. Picking up speed from its Exeter Central stop No 33 008 (later named *Eastleigh*) passes St James' Park Halt on 10 August 1976 with the 10.10 from Exeter St Davids to Waterloo. *Les Bertram*

An almost aerial view from the top of the old water tower (now demolished) at Exeter St Davids again finds Class 33 No 33 008 leaving for Waterloo, this time with the 15.55 departure on 21 July 1977. In the foreground is the GWR main line, the 1-in-37 gradient to Exeter Central all too apparent. *Brian Morrison*

As well as hauling some local services out of Exeter and longer-distance trains to Waterloo the Class 33s appeared regularly on other duties, such as the 08.48 Tavistock Junction–Fawley (in Hampshire) empty fuel tankers. Tackling the long (two-mile) climb of 1 in 42 to Hemerdon Summit, east of Plymouth, on 2 October 1979 is No 33 015. A quarter of a century later this is one freight working that is still running! *Les Bertram*

A strong lens clearly shows the steep gradient down from Exeter Central to St Davids at sunset. Opening the taps on the eight-cylinder Sulzer engine, the driver of No 33 015 darkens the sky with a departing train from Waterloo. These tough and reliable little locomotives worked the service from 1971 until 1980, when they were displaced (except on the Brighton–Exeter services) by 2,700hp Class 50s, which in turn were being displaced from the WR main line with the arrival of IC125 High Speed Train units. However, whenever a Class 50 failed or was not available Class 33s could be seen on the line, a situation that continued until the beginning of the 1990s — a stint of over 20 years! *Author*

Above: On scheduled inter-regional services working into Cornwall between the years 1969 and 1985 there was always a chance of a Class 45 or 46 'Peak' on the front end, these lengthy 1Co-Co1s adding to the variety of motive power on the Cornish rail scene. On 3 July 1981 split-headcode No 45 061 is seen approaching Menheniot with the 10.33 Newquay–Manchester. A rail-served quarry had remained open at this location until 1969. *Author*

Below: The Class 45 and 46 'Peaks' could be found on both passenger and freight trains, many arriving in Cornwall on the daily train of clay empties from Cliffe Vale, near Stoke-on-Trent. However, on 16 September 1979 Class 46 No 46 043 was in sparkling form as it breezed past Burngullow with, somewhat unusually, an up Paddington train. The locomotive was probably replaced at Plymouth North Road. Note the Drinnick Mill branch, just above the rear cab of the locomotive. *Author*

Above: Even with only six bogies in tow this Class 45 will still be working hard on the 1-in-64 climb up to Treverrin Tunnel. The train was an unusual working that started at Plymouth at 14.30 as the 2B24, arriving at Par to terminate at 15.23. The train then 'retired' to a siding before forming the 2B28 15.55 Par–Penzance stopping service *after* the 11.45 Paddington–Penzance IC125 had passed! *Author*

Below: Train 2B14 — the morning (10.22) Plymouth–Penzance, which normally comprised coaches and vans — was often hauled by one of the 1960-3 Derby/Crewe-built Class 45 'Peaks', in this case Class 45/1 No 45 150, the 2,500hp 136-tonner being seen negotiating the curves at Carlyon Bay on 21 April 1983. These fine but heavy locomotives ceased to work west of Bristol Temple Meads from October 1985. *Author*

Lostwithiel Goods Shed

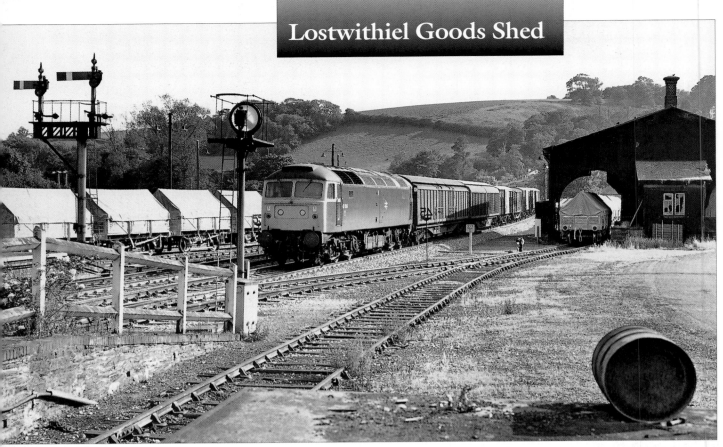

Lostwithiel up goods shed was a remarkable survivor from the pre-1892 broad-gauge era. Although not used for goods since the 1960s it remained a home for roosting pigeons and desperate railway photographers on rainy days. The sidings were used for berthing china-clay wagons, as can be seen in this 29 June 1981 view of all-blue Class 47 No 47 054 rushing past with an up air-braked freight from St Blazey. *Author*

As a result of an ill-conceived scheme to preserve it with a view to re-erecting it elsewhere, Lostwithiel goods shed was dismantled in October 1982. It is perhaps best to say (understatedly) that although the shed *was* demolished its re-erection never came to fruition, the timbers ending up as little more than firewood. Sheltering on a bleak 4 June 1981, the author was perhaps fortunate to photograph light engine No 37 271 passing Class 45/0 No 45 072 with a St Blazey–Tavistock Junction freight. *Author*

The production Class 253 units appeared in the West Country in September 1979, when the 'Cornish Riviera' and 'Golden Hind' expresses were first formed of these new 4,500hp trainsets. Although, understandably, these were unpopular with the railway-enthusiast fraternity there was no comparison in terms of performance, comfort and ride with their locomotive-and-stock predecessors. In this photograph, recorded on 19 June 1982, there appears to be IC125 infestation as No 253 029 forming the 10.25 Paddington–Penzance passes No 253 019 with the 13.35 Penzance–Paddington on Coombe Viaduct at Saltash. *Author*

Initially it was difficult to come to terms with sleek streamliners crossing 100-year-old Cornish viaducts, a sight that seemed somehow incongruous. In the lovely deciduous oak woods around Trenowth (between St Austell and Truro) lies Fal Viaduct, an 1884 structure 570ft in length and 90ft high. Of particular note is the sole remaining pier of the original Brunel viaduct, just visible below the leading power car in this 9 August 1983 view. *Author*

The IC125 units gradually took over the majority of express-train workings, and eventually even inter-regional services, releasing more locomotives for reallocation or, in most cases, withdrawal. Viewed from the top of the conveyor at Stoneycombe Quarry, between Dainton Tunnel and Aller Junction, a Class 253 descends towards Newton Abbot with an up train in August 1982 — the year the quarry sidings, visible on the left, closed. *Author*

Above: When first introduced the IC125s ran on railway infrastructure that belonged to a past age. Passing Exeter Middle signalbox at the north end of Exeter St Davids station and a myriad of lower-quadrant semaphores is unit No 253 030, forming a express from Paddington in September 1980. The units managed to reach Exeter in just a fraction over two hours from Paddington; by comparison, in 1965 a single 'Western' took 153 minutes and a pair of Class 37s 132 minutes, while in 1969 pairs of 'Warships' managed a (then) record 131 minutes 30 seconds! The difference in journey times would have been far greater had the line between Reading and Taunton been passed for sustained running at three-figure speeds. *Author*

Below: There is no doubt that the Class 253 units, marketed under the 'Inter-City 125' label, have been an enormous success. Reliability has been excellent, and none of the current generation of multiple-units begins to approach their level of passenger comfort. They say that 'what goes around comes around', and in the 21st century even the IC125s have been replaced on inter-regional trains by Virgin 'Voyagers'. Here, a quarter of a century ago at the time of writing (!), No 253 034 speeds past Langstone Rock at Dawlish Warren with a down express. *Author*

Above: It is perhaps a little impish of the author to include these two photographs after praising High Speed Train reliability, but even in the best-regulated circles problems arise. HSTs could easily operate (and indeed perform well) with just one power car functioning, but that does not take into account the South Devon banks, for which difficult stretch of line assistance is normally provided when a power car fails. On 12 July 1981 No 50 026 *Indomitable* assisted No 253 023 with the 11.40 Penzance–Paddington, seen descending Rattery Bank, west of Totnes. *Brian Morrison*

Below: This unusual event occurred in 1983, when an IC125 was declared a partial failure at Exeter St Davids and a Class 45/0 was summoned from the stabling point. Trying to make up for lost time, the combination runs fast-line through Dawlish Warren with a down Plymouth train. The IC125s' 12-cylinder Paxman engines have generally been reliable and have now covered millions of miles, but in view of their sump capacity of 35 gallons few would care to pay for an oil change! *Author*

Cornish Viaducts

There is plenty of interest in this shot of a quite delightful train passing through countryside that is pure Cornwall. The locomotive, No 50 007, was originally named *Hercules* (as here) but on 25 February 1984 would be renamed *Sir Edward Elgar*. Pictured on 18 April 1983, the Penzance–Plymouth stopping train is crossing Coombe St Stephen Viaduct, an 1886 rebuild of the original Margary Class A Brunel viaduct, the ivy-covered piers of which can still be seen on the left. After the photograph was taken the line between Burngullow and Probus (including this stretch) was singled, but in 2004 the double track was reinstated! *Author*

In recent years Liskeard's outer home signal, seen here, has been the first semaphore signal to be passed on the GWR main line from Paddington, being located at the up end of the curved Bolitho Viaduct on the down side. Crossing the curved viaduct on 18 April 1983 is a Class 47 with ballast wagons bound for the St Blazey area. *Author*

One of the most graceful viaducts in Cornwall is that at St Germans, built in 1908, when the Cornish main line was diverted onto a new alignment in this area. With small boats at anchor on the River Tiddy the down 'Cornish Riviera Express' (09.45 Paddington–Penzance) majestically crosses the structure on 11 August 1983. *Author*

Top: St Pinnock Viaduct, in the heart of the Glynn Valley, is a fine structure with nine fully buttressed piers and gothic-styled openings. Metal girders replaced the original fan-topped timber structure at the top of the piers in 1882, with the piers being heightened. At 151ft the viaduct is one of the highest in Cornwall, and in 1964 the double-track main line across the structure was singled as an economy measure, to save heavy maintenance work. No 50 027 *Lion* heads westwards with the 07.00 Exeter St Davids–Penzance. *Author*

Above: It is now many years since the Liverpool–Penzance train was locomotive-hauled but even longer since it was composed completely of Mk 1 stock. Here the 10 coaches forming the 09.36 ex-Liverpool cross Bolitho Viaduct, just to the east of Liskeard, behind No 50 034 *Furious.* Note the oil tail-lamp on the back of the BSK coach. *Author*

Above: All trains to the Torbay area now terminate at Paignton, but in days gone by some workings continued to Kingswear. (Closed by BR in 1972, this stretch of line is now home to the Paignton & Dartmouth Steam Railway.) Even those locomotive-hauled trains terminating at Paignton mostly continued into the carriage sidings at Goodrington, where the train engine would run round. An unusual visitor to the station on 5 March 1978 was No 55 003 *Meld* with the RPPR 'Deltic Ranger' railtour from Paddington. Enthusiasts savour the occasion of the first-ever 'Deltic' visit to Devon and take their photographs as the headboard is put in place for the return journey to Newton Abbot. *Author*

Top right: Few of the passengers on this train will be visiting the Torbay area to experience heavy rain, but unfortunately for them 14 September 1985 was a diabolical day. Arriving on the 'English Riviera' from Paddington is No 50 003 *Temeraire*. The line was particularly busy on summer Saturdays, when thousands of holidaymakers would arrive from London, the Midlands and the North of England, but during the winter months, especially off-peak, the station was (and still is) very quiet indeed. *Author*

Lower right: The 'Westerns' last summer, that of 1976, was one of the driest and hottest on record, and restrictions were placed upon the washing of rolling stock and locomotives. Looking in very poor condition externally and with its well-worn Maybach engines smoking profusely, No 1023 *Western Fusilier* awaits the 'off' for Paddington as welcome (from a gardener's perspective!) pouring rain evaporates from its warm roof. *Author*

Snow!

Above: Heavy snow is a comparative rarity in Cornwall, other than on the highest moorland. However, on the evening of 18 January 1985 snow was forecast, prompting a hasty decision by the author to travel as a 'waker' on the Paddington–Penzance sleeping-car train, alighting at Par. One of the first up trains on the 19th was this Paddington-bound IC125 unit. Station staff are clearing the platforms for passengers. *Author*

Below: After a session at Par the short journey to Bodmin Road (now Parkway) was undertaken. With settled snow lending the conifers and surrounding countryside an almost Tyrolean look, No 47 600 accelerates the 09.32 Penzance–Paddington away from the station and attacks the steep climb to Doublebois. Fortunately the locomotive was fitted with electric train heating. *Author*

Above: On some roads traffic was affected by the inclement conditions, but the trains continued to run to schedule, at least on the up line. There was plenty of snow on the ground at Liskeard, and points had to be cleared manually. With the unusual short starting signal 'off' and with the driver looking back to check that everybody is on board and that doors are closed, No 47 491 prepares to depart with the 10.50 Penzance–Brighton train. *Author*

Below: A 'bubble' in the snow at Liskeard as car No W55025 arrives at the branch terminus with the 12.07 from Looe, also on 19 January 1985. Within just over a year the DMUs would be replaced (temporarily, as it turned out) by two-car Class 142 units that proved not up to the job, but that is beyond the scope of this book, other than to say that the diesel-mechanicals later reappeared. *Author*

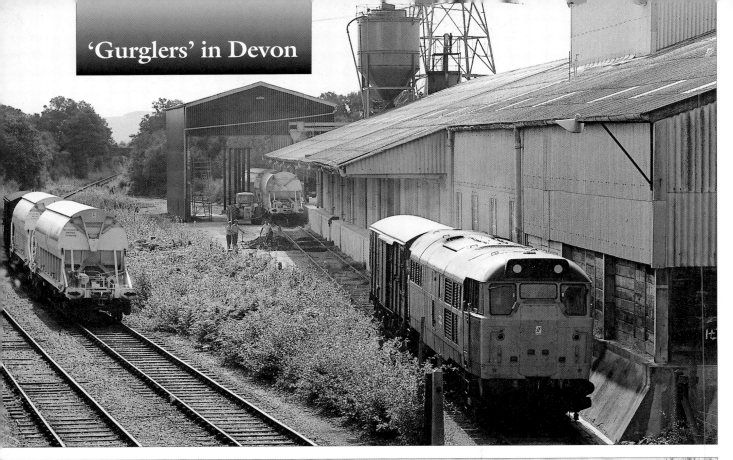

Top left: This busy scene, recorded on 31 August 1982, features the ECC ball-clay works at Heathfield, at the end of the truncated Moretonhampstead branch. Class 31 No 31 118 is engaged in a complicated shunt, removing loaded 'Tiger' wagons and vans and replacing them with empties before returning to Newton Abbot. *David H. Mitchell*

Lower left: Although two pictures of Class 31s on clay trains are included, in the author's experience photographs of such occurrences were difficult to come by in Devon and impossible in Cornwall. However, on 22 March 1982 Dave Mitchell was on hand at Barnstaple to record No 31 286 returning from Marland via Torrington with just five wagons of ball clay. The erstwhile Barnstaple Junction had been the terminus for passenger trains since October 1970, when the Ilfracombe line closed. *David H. Mitchell*

Top right: A powerful picture of double-headed Class 31s, Nos 31 118 and 31 124, passing Dawlish with a freight from Exeter Riverside to Tavistock Junction, Plymouth, on 30 August 1979. There is no doubt that although photographs on the famous sea wall are hackneyed the location does give excellent views of the railway in action, without intrusion from trees and other foliage. *A. O. Wynn*

Lower right: Descending the steep gradient from Exeter Central to Exeter St Davids on 13 July 1976 is a Yeovil Junction–Meldon Quarry working. Class 31 No 31 209 has a goodly number of mixed ballast wagons behind it, but these being empty the train weight will be modest. This locomotive was built in 1960, yet 44 years later these 1,470hp all-rounders could still be seen at Yeovil on certain summer-dated trains between Bristol and Weymouth! *Brian Morrison*

5,400hp!

Above: A single Class 50 could be impressive, but couple two together and work them in multiple, thereby unleashing 5,400hp, and the motive-power show really started. A regular candidate for a brace of 'Hoovers' was train 3S15 Penzance–Glasgow parcels. Storming through Liskeard on 22 April 1983 are Nos 50 005 *Collingwood* and 50 009 *Conqueror.* The down buildings on the left would later be demolished and replaced by a featureless concrete shelter. *Author*

Below: Almost worthy of a 0-60mph rating, the combination of a pair of Class 50s and just three Mk 1 coaches was the exciting prospect that greeted the photographer at Liskeard on 5 February 1983 as Nos 50 040 *Leviathan* and 50 028 *Lion* powered the 11.05 Penzance– Plymouth local. Either one of the locomotives was on test following depot attention or there was surplus motive power at Penzance. *Author*

Above: A train that regularly attracted a mixture of passenger coaches and vans was the 13.45 Penzance–Plymouth parcels, which included the stock off the 10.20 Plymouth–Penzance local. On 2 June 1981 the working produced this Class 50 pairing — No 50 028 *Tiger* in all-blue livery and No 50 003 *Temeraire* in 'large logo' style. The formation is crossing Gover Viaduct, between Burngullow and St Austell. *Author*

Below: There are some fascinating old mine workings under the track at Lower Dowgas Farm, a few miles west of Burngullow. At this location the track is braced, and in this view the special rods can just be seen beside the running rails. The heavy 12.10 Penzance–Glasgow parcels needs all the power it can get up the 1-in-84/70 climb to Burngullow on 18 April 1983, Nos 50 047 *Swiftsure* and 50 045 *Achilles* duly obliging. *Author*

The Invaders

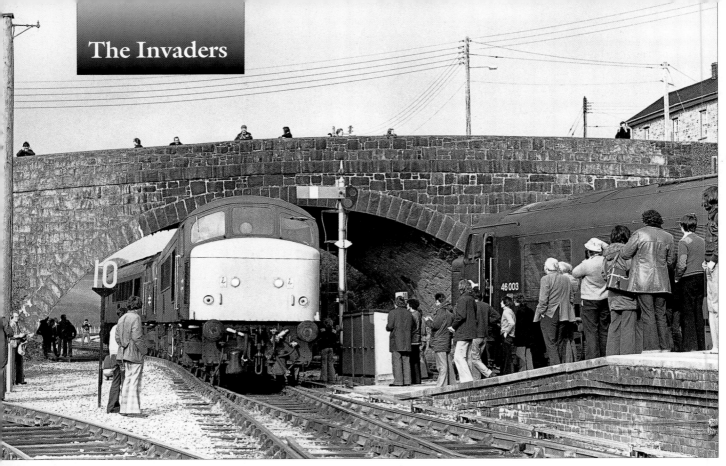

Above: It was a really tough task to photograph three Class 46 'Peaks' in Cornwall in a single frame, but on 5 March 1978 such an opportunity occurred at Par, junction for Newquay. Having replaced Class 55 No 55 003 with Class 46 No 46 003 at Newton Abbot, RPPR had run its 'Deltic Ranger' tour westward and into Cornwall. As the train was waiting to return from Par Nos 46 009 and 46 014 worked towards St Blazey depot 'light engine', much to the delight of participants. *Author*

Below: Class 31s did get as far as Cornwall, but such workings were exceptional; as mentioned elsewhere, in more than 100 visits made by the author to the Duchy between 1969 and 2004 — many of them for up to a week rather than a single day — this was the only example ever seen. Having worked an early-morning freight to St Blazey on 3 June 1981, No 31 273 worked back to base 'light engine'. The interloper is pictured passing Bodmin Road. *Author*

It was only towards the end of their time on BR that Class 40s worked into Devon and Cornwall, at the head of enthusiast specials. Coach 'A' was always in demand by those whose enthusiasm was perhaps physically demonstrable, but in the case of the F&W Railtours 'Western Whistler' two coaches seem to be full of 'bellowers'. No 40 025 *Lusitania* leaves Totnes and prepares to attack the 1-in-66/71/47 of Rattery Bank on 19 September 1982. *Author*

It seems rather fitting to end our extensive tour of the counties of Devon and Cornwall in the 'Diesel Days' at the buffer-stops under the overall roof at Penzance. This unique invader, green-liveried 2,000hp Class 40 No 40 122, originally numbered D200 and introduced in March 1958, had worked the 'Penzance Fryer' railtour from Manchester to Penzance on 9 November 1985 — towards the end of the last year covered in this (approximately) 1951-85 review. They were great years, and the author hopes this book will enable the reader to wallow in some modern-traction nostalgia while savouring the early diesel era in this magnificent part of the world, all under the auspices of good old 'British Railways'! *Author*

Acknowledgements

I should like to express my sincere gratitude to all of the photographers who contributed to *Diesel Days: Devon and Cornwall*, and a photographic credit or source is shown after every caption. However, a number of photographers made special efforts to meet my requirements, and in no particular order I should like to record my special thanks to: Peter Treloar, Geoff Gillham, Maurice Dart, Michael Mensing, Brian Morrison, Colin Marsden and the Stephenson Locomotive Society. Finally I should like to thank my old friend John Hicks, who has travelled with me on so many railway photographic expeditions to Devon and Cornwall over the past three decades, for his loyal friendship. We had some truly memorable times and plenty of chuckles, but sadly many of the sights and sounds we experienced and the people we met along the way have gone forever. This book is dedicated to John, a true friend.

Bibliography

Baker, S. K.
Rail Atlas Great Britain & Northern Ireland
(various editions) — Oxford Publishing Co

Binding, John
Brunel's Cornish Viaducts
— Atlantic Publishing/Pendragon Books/HMRS, 1993

Dart, M.
The Last Days of Steam in Devon and Plymouth
and *The Last Days of Steam in Cornwall*
— Alan Sutton Publishing, 1991

Daniels, Gerald, and Dench, Les
Passengers No More — Ian Allan, 1980

Marsden, Colin J.
35 Years of Main Line Diesel Traction
— Oxford Publishing Co, 1982
BR Locomotive Renumbering — Ian Allan, 1984

Morrison, Brian
BR DMUs and Diesel Railcars — Ian Allan, 1998

Reed, Brian
Diesel-Hydraulic Locomotives of the Western Region
— David & Charles, 1974

Vaughan, John
Western Diesels in Camera — Ian Allan, 1977
The Power of the 50s — Oxford Publishing Co, 1979
Railtour Pictorial — Railway Pictorial Publications, 1979
Diesels on the Western Region — Ian Allan, 1982
Diesels in the Duchy — Ian Allan, 1983
West Country China Clay Trains (two editions)
— Oxford Publishing Co, 1987 and 1999
The Newquay Branch and its Branches
— Oxford Publishing Co, 1991
Branches & Byways: Cornwall — Oxford Publishing Co, 2002

Various issues of Ian Allan 'ABCs' and BR Working Timetables (Western Region)

Following our photographic railtour of Devon and Cornwall it is difficult to believe, on reflection, that so many classes of diesel locomotive, types of railway carriage and examples of goods wagon no longer run on our railway network. Infrastructure has changed out of all recognition, with the abolition of signalboxes and their associated signals, the modernisation of stations and the simplification of trackwork and layout, as well as the complete closure of lines. The loss of much of the freight traffic has also been a grievous loss to our railways. Train liveries have undergone bewildering changes, and even British Railways itself has given way to a complex structure of track owners, stock owners, operating companies and franchisees. Other than for the scrapping of locomotives (especially the WR diesel-hydraulics!) the saddest episode has been the closure of complete railway lines, such as the old Carbis Wharf line from Bugle in Cornwall, seen here. This 1982-built 80-ton 'Tiger' PBA wagon, containing 57 tons of china clay, waits at Carbis for collection and its long monthly journey to Scotland. By the end of the decade the weeds would take over completely as yet another branch line closed forever and another freight flow was lost. This volume provides a permanent record of a fascinating era — the early 'Diesel Days' in Devon and Cornwall. *John Vaughan*

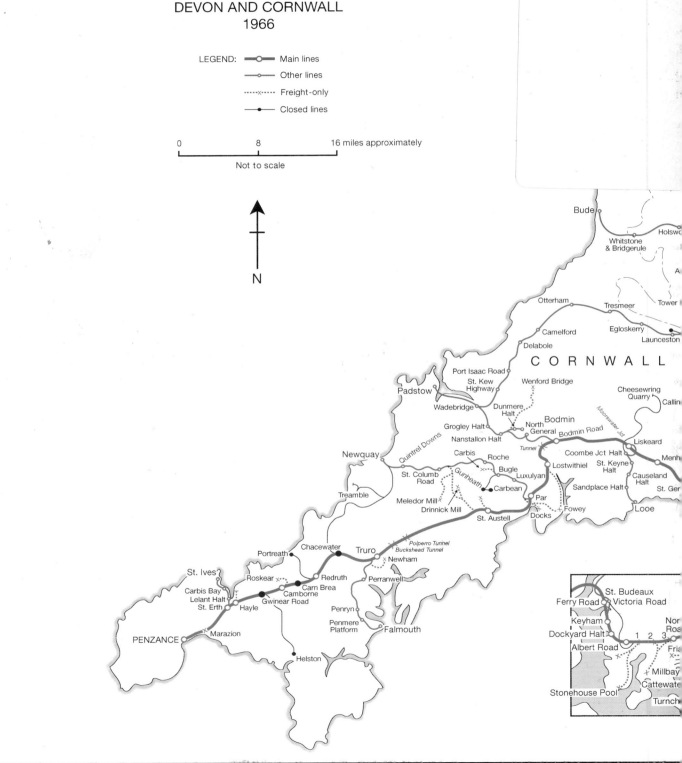

BRITISH RAILWAYS
DEVON AND CORNWALL
1966

LEGEND:
- ══○══ Main lines
- ──○── Other lines
- ····×···· Freight-only
- ──●── Closed lines

0   8   16 miles approximately

Not to scale

N

C O R N W A L L

Bude
Holswo
Whitstone & Bridgerule
Tower
Otterham
Tresmeer
Camelford
Egloskerry
Launceston
Delabole
Port Isaac Road
St. Kew Highway
Wenford Bridge
Cheesewring Quarry
Callin
Padstow
Wadebridge
Dunmere Halt
Bodmin
North General
Bodmin Road
Moorswater Jct
Liskeard
Grogley Halt
Nanstallon Halt
Carbis
Roche
Tunnel
Coombe Jct Halt
Menh
Newquay
Quintrel Downs
Bugle
Luxulyan
Lostwithiel
St. Keyne Halt
St. Columb Road
Gunheath
Carbean
Sandplace Halt
Causeland Halt
St. Ger
Treamble
Meledor Mill
Drinnick Mill
Par
Fowey
Looe
Docks
St. Austell
Polperro Tunnel
Buckshead Tunnel
Chacewater
Truro
Portreath
Newham
St. Ives
Roskear
Redruth
Newham
Perranwell
St. Budeaux
Carbis Bay
Lelant Halt
Carn Brea
Camborne
Gwinear Road
Ferry Road
Victoria Road
St. Erth
Hayle
Penryn
Keyham
Nor Roa
PENZANCE
Marazion
Penmere Platform
Falmouth
Dockyard Halt
1 2 3
Albert Road
Fria
Helston
Millbay
Stonehouse Pool
Cattewate
Turnch